THE
JEWISH
HOLIDAY
COOK BOOK

Also by Leah W. Leonard

JEWISH COOKERY

THE

JEWISH

HOLIDAY

COOK BOOK

By Leah W. Leonard

GRAMERCY PUBLISHING COMPANY • NEW YORK

*This edition published by Gramercy
Publishing Company, a division
of Crown Publishers, Inc.*

C   D   E   F   G   H

Acknowledgments

My deepest appreciation goes to the countless readers of my weekly column, "Foods to Remember," an American Jewish Press Feature, for their invaluable suggestions as well as letters of appreciation.

Thanks to relatives and friends for sharing "heirloom recipes" with my readers.

My sincere appreciation for a graphic description of *Tu b'Sh'vat* celebrations in Israel goes to the charming Rachel, Israeli wife of Rabbi Mayer Abramowitz of Miami Beach, Florida.

To Mrs. Harold Shapiro, wife of the Mayor of Miami Beach, Florida, thanks and appreciation for a "Sabra's" view of Israeli food customs.*

For enthusiastic encouragement and practical assistance in planning this book, sincere thanks and appreciation to Herbert Michelman of Crown Publishers.

Last but not least, gratitude to Oscar Leonard, for cheerfully submitting to trials and errors in the testing of recipes herewith included for the first time with husbandly approval.

* Native-born Israelis are commonly called Sabras. A Sabra is the prickly pear type of fruit of the cactus plant, tough and unapproachable from the outside but very tender within.

Preface

Just as the art of cooking depends on the ingenuity and resources of the home-maker to make it truly *The Eighth Art,* the celebrations of Jewish holidays and festivals, as well as family celebrations from "Mazel Tov" at birth to "Mazel Tov" at weddings, are the privilege and province of the home engineer.

And as food customs for all celebrations are a factor in the continuity of a people, the suggestions for menus and recipes in the following pages are the result of very careful planning and consideration of preparation time as well as budgetary resources and traditional food customs.

Where the services of a caterer are available, there is no necessity beyond special demands of the family and friends or participants in celebrations in or out of the home. However, the knowledge of appropriate menus as well as special items of food to suit the occasion is welcome equipment. Careful thought has also been given to sections in this book which may be turned over to professional service.

All recipes in this book are in accordance with Jewish Dietary Laws.
In the preparation of menus for various occasions, due consideration has been given to *fleishig, milchig,* and *pareve* alternatives and variations.
All measurements of ingredients are level and standard.

The Hebrew Calendar

According to ancient custom, the Hebrew calendar is based on lunar calculations. The first of each month is called Rosh Chodesh, or "head" (beginning) of the month.

The ordinary year is divided into 12 months, 355 days, some months having 29 days and some 30 days.

Leap Year, called in Yiddish "eeber yor," has 13 months. The thirteenth month is called "Adar Shani" in Hebrew, meaning "second Adar" which follows the first "Adar," before the month of "Nissan."

Because of this difference of a whole month instead of one day in leap years of the Hebrew calendar and the calendar used according to the Common Era, Jewish holidays do not fall on the same days of the latter calendar each year. Here is a listing of the months of the Hebrew Calendar:

1st	month,	Tishri	7th	month,	Nissan
2nd	"	Heshvan	8th	"	Iyar
3rd	"	Kislev	9th	"	Sivan
4th	"	Tebet (Tevas)	10th	"	Tammuz
5th	"	Sh'vat	11th	"	Ab or Ov
6th	"	Adar	12th	"	Ellul

Table of Contents

Jewish Holidays and Food Associations

Holiday	Hebrew Date	Month, C.E.	Traditional Foods
Rosh Hashonah (New Year)	Tishri 1, 2	Sept. or Oct.	Honey and Apple, Honey Cake, Tzimmes of Carrots
Yom Kippur (Day of Atonement)	Tishri 10	Sept. or Oct.	Total abstinence from food
Succoth	Tishri 15 to 23	October	Holishkes (Praakes), Kreplach, Shtrudel
Channukah	Kislev 25 to Tebet 2	December	Grated Potato Latkes, Potato Kugel
Chamisho Oser b'Sh'vat (Tu b'Sh'vat)	Sh'vat 15	January	Bokser (St. John's Bread), Almonds, Raisins, Fruits grown in Israel
Purim	Adar 14	March	Hamantaschen, Nahit, Apples, Nuts, Raisins, Wine
Pesach (Passover)	Nissan 14 to 22	April	Matzo, Matzo products, Chremzlach, Nuts, Wine
Lag b'Omer	Iyar 18	May	B'ob (Favah Beans or Broad Beans) Spring fruits
Shevuoth	Sivan 6, 7	May	Cheese Blintzes, Cheese Kreplach, Dairy Foods

SABBATH, TRADITIONAL DAY OF REST

The Sabbath Day has been called by thoughtful persons "the noblest holiday of the Jewish calendar." It is the day of rest from all labor. The Fourth Commandment is the first injunction in recorded history making one day in seven a compulsory rest day. It has taken many centuries of modern civilization to achieve such legislation on behalf of those who labor "and earn their bread in the sweat of their brow."

Because all work on the Sabbath Day is forbidden, the home-maker also takes a holiday from the culinary department of the home. Careful planning makes the preparation of foods on Friday a joy instead of a chore. Thanks to advancements in the techniques of food processing, storage, handling and marketing, the strictly kosher kitchen can be supplied with every Sabbath need from the corner foodshop or chain store which carries kosher foods in special departments. Quick frozen meats and poultry, *kashered* and ready for thawing and cooking, are available to modest-income families, direct from the foodshop or in desired quantities for home storage in the frozen food cabinet or compartment of the refrigerator. Some enterprising companies even ship frozen meats and poultry to outlying sections of the country.

Gefilte Fish, which required hours of preparation in Grandmother's day, can be had in glass containers for immediate use, or made in the modern manner, thanks to the pressure cooker, in an efficiency kitchenette apartment. And if an accommodating as well as enterprising fish marketer is in the neighborhood, fish is cleaned, filleted and put through the grinder for grateful customers.

Baked foods, from Challah (Sabbath loaf) to Shtrudel and a large variety of cakes, are no longer time-consuming kitchen rituals, even for those who cherish the fragrance of home-baked bread and cake. In addition to the convenience of professionally baked Challah and other bakery items, there is an ever-increasing variety of prepared "mixes" which can be kept on the pantry shelf for quick and easy conversion into delicacies undreamed of in ages past.

However, the following pages of suggested menus and recipes for customary Sabbath foods will serve as a guide to the novice as well as to the experienced home-maker in making the Sabbath Day one of joy as well as freedom from labor.

Suggested Menus for Friday Night

MENU 1
Gefilte Fish with Horseradish
Chicken Soup with Noodles
Chicken with Bread Crumb and
Giblet Dressing
Peas and Carrots
Greens Salad with French Dressing
Hot or Cold Beverage
Cake or Cookies

MENU 2
Chopped Beef Liver Canapés
Chilled Tomato Juice
Roast Turkey with Dressing
Green Beans and Almonds
Raw Carrot Salad
Hot or Cold Beverage
Sponge Cake or Cookies

MENU 3
Gefilte Fish
Chicken Soup with Mandlen
Stewed Chicken with Limas
Applesauce
Tossed Greens Salad
Hot or Cold Beverage
Cake or Cookies

MENU 4
Broiled Grapefruit Halves
Gefilte Fish, Beet Salad
Veal Breast, Chopped Beef Filling
Browned Potatoes
Cabbage and Cranberry Slaw
Hot or Cold Beverage
Hazelnut Cookies

MENU 5
Mock Gefilte Fish
Chicken Soup with Mandlen
or Farfel
Fresh, Frozen or Canned
Green Beans
Tomato and/or Cucumber Salad
Hot or Cold Beverage
Dried Fruit Compote or
Melon in Season

MENU 6
Gefilte Fish, Pickled Beet Relish
Sliced Cold Turkey, Sweet Potatoes
Green Beans and Almonds
Hot or Cold Beverage
Shtrudel

MENU 7
Fresh Caviar (Icre de Carp)
Broiled Fish Patties
Oven-Broiled Chicken
Cauliflower or Asparagus
Tomato, Lettuce Salad
Hot or Cold Beverage
Fresh Fruit or Berries in Season

MENU 8
Fruit Cup
Pickled Smelts
Roast Shoulder of Lamb
Risi-Bisi (Rice and Peas)
Tossed Greens Salad
Hot or Cold Beverage
Cookies

Suggested Menus for Sabbath

MENU 1
Gefilte Fish
Cholent
Carrot and Pineapple Ring
Hot or Cold Beverage
Cake or Cookies

MENU 2
Pickled Smelts
Roast Turkey with Dressing
Green Beans and Almonds
Raw Carrot Salad
Hot or Cold Beverage
Sponge Cake

MENU 3
Fresh Caviar (Icre de Carp)
Potted Roast of Lamb Shoulder
Beet Salad
Hot or Cold Beverage
Shabbos Kugel

MENU 4
Grapefruit
Gefilte Fish
Veal Breast, Chopped Beef Filling
Browned Potatoes
Cole Slaw
Hot or Cold Beverage
Nut Fingers

MENU 5
Herring in Wine Sauce
Oven-Broiled Chicken
Risi-Bisi
Tomato, Cucumber Salad
Hot or Cold Beverage
Honey Cake

MENU 9
Fruit Cup

Chopped Beef Liver Canapés
Roast Shoulder of Lamb
Mashed Potatoes
Tossed Greens Salad
Hot or Cold Beverage
Date Drops

MENU 6
Chopped Beef Liver on Lettuce
Chicken Fricassee
Upside-down Pineapple-
Noodle Kugel
Hot or Cold Beverage
Fruit Salad, Cookies

MENU 7
Gefilte Fish
Roast Chicken with Dressing
Uncooked Cranberry, Apple
and Nut Relish
Tomato Salad
Hot or Cold Beverage
Shtrudel

MENU 8
Gefilte Fish Ball Canapés
Stewed Chicken with Limas
Asparagus Tips Salad
Hot or Cold Beverage
Stewed Dried Fruit, Cookies

MENU 10
Gefilte Fish Ball Canapés
Sweet-Sour Fish
Potato Salad
Sunburst Salad
Hot or Cold Beverage
Upside-down Pineapple-
Noodle Kugel

Challah, wine, fruits in season are distinctly Sabbath items.

HOMEMADE CHALLAH (Sabbath Loaf)

2 packages yeast, cake or granulated
¼ cup lukewarm water
1 teaspoon sugar
6 cups all-purpose flour
1 tablespoon salt

3 eggs
4 tablespoons vegetable shortening or oil
2 tablespoons sugar
2 cups hot water (or liquid
  drained from potatoes)
a pinch of saffron

Dissolve yeast in lukewarm water, sweetened with the teaspoon of sugar to hasten yeast action. Sift together flour and salt into a large mixing bowl and make a well in the center. Stir in the dissolved yeast in center of flour, cover and let stand while preparing the rest of the ingredients. Beat eggs in another bowl. Combine vegetable shortening or oil, sugar and hot water to which the saffron (purchased in any drugstore or herb shop) has been added and let cool to lukewarm. Now stir into the partly risen yeast mixture in center of flour the beaten eggs and lukewarm mixture alternately, till a ball of dough is formed. Turn out on a floured kneading board and knead thoroughly till the dough becomes smooth and elastic.

Return the ball of dough to bowl, brush top with a little shortening or oil, dust with flour and cover with a double thickness of towel. Place in a warm place away from draughts till risen to double in bulk. Knead again and divide in two parts for two loaves. Cut each half into three portions and roll between palms and kneading board to make equal lengths for braiding. Braid loosely, pinching each of the ends together securely. Place both loaves on a lightly greased and floured baking pan. Cover and let rise again till double in bulk, approximately 1½ hours. Brush tops with diluted egg yolk for a gloss and bake 15 minutes at 400°, reduce heat to 375° and bake 45 minutes longer or till nicely browned on bottom.

Yields 2 braided loaves.

Variations: Reserve a ball of dough from each portion after dividing dough into two parts. Use this for making thin braids to place on top of each loaf after brushing with diluted egg yolk. Brush top of the thin braid also, if desired. Or form bits of dough to resemble little birds to place on top of braided loaves. Or form a Jacob's Ladder by placing pencil-thin strips on top of loaves. Be sure to let rise before baking the decorated loaves. Adding a sprinkling of poppyseeds over tops of loaves is customary. Or a few sesame seeds may be used in the same manner, which is the favorite in many European countries as well as in Israel. The seeds will adhere if sprinkled on while the diluted egg yolk is moist.

LOAF PAN CHALLAH

Braid the two loaves loosely and fit each into a 9 x 4-inch lightly greased and floured loaf pan. Let rise as in basic recipe and proceed in the same manner for decorating and baking. This form of loaf is sometimes preferred because it is easier to slice for sandwiches or toast during the week.

EASY-WAY GEFILTE FISH (Pressure Cooker Method)

3 pounds fresh fish (any firm-fleshed variety like carp, yellow pike, buffalo—or combination of any two varieties)
2 large onions
2 carrots

2 stalks celery and leaves
2 slices white bread (or ½ cup crumbs)
2 eggs
salt and pepper to taste
parsley
cold water as directed

If the fish market does not clean and fillet the fish for you, be sure to remove scales thoroughly. Remove eyes and gills from the head. Cut away fins. Slit open the fish and remove entrails. Wash under cold running water. Cut off head, split it and place in the bottom of the pressure cooker, cut side down. Add 1 diced or sliced onion and 1 sliced carrot. Add diced celery and minced leaves. Now remove the flesh from the skin and bones of the fish. This can be handled best by cutting the fish into portions first. If desired, the prepared fish pulp can be stuffed back into the portions between skin and bone section. Put the filleted fish through the food chopper, using the fine cutter. To the pulp add the remaining onion and carrot, grated, soaked and squeezed bread or crumbs, eggs, salt and pepper to taste. Mix thoroughly to form a thick pulp.

Wet the hands in cold water and either fill the skin and bone sections with the pulp or form the mixture into balls of desired size. Place the trivet over the head, bones and vegetables in the pot, then arrange the fish balls or portions on the trivet. Add enough cold water to come up to the fish balls, or as directed with your make of pressure cooker. Cover and adjust the pressure gauge to 10 pounds pressure. Cook over moderate heat until the gauge begins to "jiggle," then turn down heat as per directions and cook 10 to 12 minutes. Turn off heat and let stand 2 minutes before reducing the heat of the pot under cold running water. Remove the gauge to let remaining steam escape. Remove cover and let the cooked fish stand for 10 to 15 minutes before lifting out the balls or stuffed sections to a bowl or platter for storage in the refrigerator. Place a slice of the carrot on top of each portion of fish, pressing it in lightly with the finger. Arrange pieces of carrot around the cooked fish. Put the liquid or sauce through a strainer over the fish or in a separate dish for chilling, cutting and adding as garnish, with parsley sprigs just before serving. Wedges or slices of lemon make additional garnish if desired.

Serves 6 or more.

GEFILTE FISH (Traditional Method)

Prepare the fish (as in above recipe) and form into balls or stuff back into sections. Place these over head, bones and vegetables as per above recipe. Add cold water barely to cover and cook over moderate heat, allowing 1½ to 2 hours of slow simmering after the contents are brought to a boil. Be sure to let the fish cool in the pot before removing to storage bowl or platter. Straining the liquid or sauce over the cooked fish is one way of doing it. The other method is to strain the liquid into a separate dish and then cutting it into squares after it has chilled and jelled. Garnish as suggested if desired. Or serve plain with horseradish colored red with beet juice.

Note: Horseradish, plain or beet-colored, is available in almost every chain store and food market. If the plain product only is at hand, add a little grated cooked or canned beets and the red liquid to achieve the desired color.

BAKED GEFILTE FISH

3 pounds filleted and chopped fish (combinations of any two firm-fleshed fish like carp, pike, buffalo, perch, etc.)
1 tablespoon salt
¼ teaspoon white or black ground pepper
1 large onion, peeled and grated

1 large carrot, scraped and grated
2 stalks celery, diced and chopped with fish
2 slices stale white bread or Challah, soaked in cold water and squeezed dry
3 eggs

Fillet fresh fish, removing flesh from bones and skin, then put through food grinder using medium blade. Or chop in a wooden bowl to form a compact pulp. Add the other ingredients in the order listed and combine thoroughly. Taste and add seasoning if necessary or to suit the taste. Remember that matzo may be substituted for the equivalent amount of bread. Line loaf pans with aluminum foil and fill half full with the fish pulp, patting down to achieve a smooth top. Bake in a preheated oven 35 to 40 minutes at 350° or till nicely browned on top. Invert pans and peel off the foil. Let cool or chill before slicing into serving portions. Arrange on lettuce or other greens, garnish with parsley, lemon wedges, radish roses, to suit the occasion and the imagination.

Serves 6 to 8.

BROILED FISH PATTIES

The prepared fish pulp (as in above recipe) may be formed into 1½-inch thick rolls or individual round patties a half inch thick and 1½ to 2 inches in diameter. Roll or dust with fine cracker crumbs or matzo meal and place these on a lightly greased (butter or substitute) cookie sheet or shallow baking pan and slip under the broiler flame 10 minutes at 350° or till lightly browned on top. Turn to brown lightly on other side. Let cool or chill before serving, garnished to suit the taste.

MOCK GEFILTE FISH (Salmon Balls)

1 tall can salmon, drained, liquid saved
1 onion, grated
1 carrot, grated

3 eggs, separated
4 tablespoons cracker or bread crumbs or matzo meal
salt and pepper to taste

Combine the drained salmon, grated onion and carrot by mixing with a fork. Add egg yolks and stir well. Stir in crumbs or matzo meal and season to taste with salt and pepper. Beat egg whites stiff and fold into the mixture. Let stand while preparing the sauce as follows:

Sauce

2 onions, sliced
2 carrots, diced or sliced
liquid drained from canned salmon plus cold water to make 4 cups

½ teaspoon sugar
minced parsley, optional

Combine the above ingredients and bring to a boil. Reduce heat and let simmer a few minutes. Form the fish mixture into balls the size of walnuts and drop these one by one into the sauce. Cook uncovered at a slow simmer for 45 minutes. *Cover, turn off heat and let the contents of pot cool before lifting lid and removing the fish balls to a platter or serving plate.* Garnish with some of the cooked carrot slices. Strain the sauce over the fish balls. Chill well and garnish with parsley, sliced lemon or sliced hard-cooked eggs. Serve with baked potatoes on the half shell.

Serves 4.

BOILED FISH WITH EGG SAUCE

3 pounds fish, cleaned and cut into 6 portions	6 peppercorns
1 carrot	2 tablespoons lemon juice
1 parsnip	2 teaspoons salt
2 stalks celery, leaves included	a dash of white pepper
1 large onion, sliced	3 eggs
3 bay leaves	garnish of lemon slices or wedges, parsley

Use the head of fish. Remove gills and eyes, split it and place cut side down in bottom of the pot to be used. Scrape the carrot and parsnip and slice or dice. Cut celery into ½-inch pieces. Add these and the onion slices to the fish head, arranging the vegetables around and on top. Place the cut portions of fish on top of vegetables, add cold water to come half-way up the portions of fish and add bay leaves, peppercorns, lemon juice, salt and pepper. Place over moderate heat until the liquid begins to bubble. Reduce heat and simmer the fish 15 to 20 minutes. The fish must not cook to the point where the flesh separates from the bones. Remove from heat.

Lift fish portions carefully to a platter. Strain the fish liquid into another pot or saucepan and bring to a boil. Beat eggs with rotary beater and stir the boiling hot fish sauce into the beaten eggs, stirring rapidly while pouring until the sauce is thickened. Pour over fish or serve separately. Garnish with lemon and parsley.

Serves 6.

SWEET-SOUR FISH (Family Style)

3 pounds fresh fish, dressed and cut (pike, pickerel, white fish or bass)	3 bay leaves
	12 peppercorns
2 tablespoons salt	½ cup cider vinegar
1 large onion, sliced or diced	½ cup brown sugar
1 carrot, sliced	10 gingersnaps
	¼ cup seedless raisins, optional
	1 lemon, sliced fine

Sprinkle all sides of fish portions with salt and let stand in a covered glass container in the refrigerator at least 2 hours. Wash and drain fish thoroughly and arrange in cooking pot with the onion and carrot slices between pieces. Add cold water to come even with top of fish and cook, uncovered, over moderate heat, allowing 10 to 12 minutes per pound. Add bay leaves, peppercorns, vinegar, sugar, gingersnaps and raisins and let cook, covered, 10 minutes longer. Let cool before lifting out fish portions to a serving platter. Strain the gravy over fish and garnish with thinly sliced lemon. Best when chilled before serving.

Serves 8 to 10.

FRESH CAVIAR, RUMANIAN STYLE (Icre de Carp)

1 pound fresh carp roe
1 tablespoon salt
½ cup lemon juice
½ cup olive oil (or salad oil)

a dash of garlic powder, optional
minced parsley for garnish
lettuce
black olives (Maslinas)

Sprinkle the fresh carp roe with salt and let stand in a covered glass dish in the refrigerator overnight. Rinse with cold water and remove as much of the membrane as possible. Beat with a silver fork or rotary beater in a deep mixing bowl, adding the lemon juice and oil alternately a little at a time while continuing to beat till thick enough to hold a peak. The remaining membrane will cling to the tines of the fork or the beater and can be removed easily. The thickened "icre," as it is called by Rumanians, will be light-colored. Fold in a dash of garlic powder if desired and sprinkle with minced parsley for color. Serve on lettuce and garnish with black olives, called Maslinas. Or spread on fingers of pumpernickle or salted crackers and sprinkle with minced parsley, paprika or fresh dill, and serve with wine or cocktails.

As an appetizer this amount will serve 8 to 10.

CHOPPED BEEF LIVER (Basic Recipe)

1 pound beef liver
1 onion
3 tablespoons chicken fat or
vegetable shortening

2 hard-cooked eggs
minced parsley

Broil sliced liver under a hot broiler flame, turning slices as soon as seared, to brown lightly on under side. Let cool before removing veins and outer skin. Brown diced onion in fat. Put cut liver, hard-cooked eggs and browned onions through food chopper or chop to a smooth paste in a wooden bowl. Add minced parsley. Season to taste. Chill.

Serves 8 to 10.

Variation 1: Add 1 uncooked egg after chopping. Blend well, then add minced green celery leaves and parsley. Grease the inside of a bowl and pack in the chopped liver. Chill at least 1 hour before unmolding on a bed of lettuce.

Variation 2: To each pound of liver add ½ cup of peanut butter. Proceed as in basic recipe and blend in the peanut butter with the minced greens.

CHOLENT

2 large onions, diced	1½ pounds potatoes, cubed
2 tablespoons schmaltz or oil	½ pound lima beans, soaked
2½ to 3½ pounds beef (brisket,	overnight
short ribs, chuck)	boiling water to cover
2 tablespoons flour seasoned with	1 medium-size carrot, diced or
salt and pepper or paprika	grated, optional
	1 small turnip, diced, optional

Sauté diced onions in hot fat in a heavy pot or Dutch oven till yellow or lightly browned. Sear meat on all sides and sprinkle with seasoned flour. Add potatoes, soaked beans, water to cover and the other vegetables, if used. Bring to a boil, skim, cover tightly and let simmer 3 to 4 hours on top of stove. Lift cover to make certain there is adequate liquid in the pot. If possible let the Cholent bake in a very low heated oven, 200°, overnight or till ready to serve on the Sabbath. Or place the covered pot on an asbestos pad or old-fashioned stove lid over the pilot light for slow cooking overnight.

When done the potatoes, meat, beans and gravy should be a rich red-brown and the aroma heavenly, or *tahm gan Eden* (taste of Paradise). If you have the privilege of using your neighborhood baker's oven, brick or tile, results will be truly traditional. Sending the *Shabbos goy* (non-Jewish servant) for the Cholent on Sabbath is part of the tradition. Serves 6.

BROWN GROATS AND NAVY BEANS CHOLENT

2½ to 3 pounds brisket of beef	1 cup brown buckwheat groats,
1 large onion, peeled and diced	coarse or medium
fine	1 cup navy beans
1 cup grated raw carrot, optional	1 tablespoon salt
1 cup chopped or finely diced	1 large clove garlic or ¼ tea-
celery, including leaves	spoon garlic salt
	boiling water to cover

Sear the meat in a large heavy pot, fitted with a cover, until well browned on all sides. Add the onion, carrot and celery, stirring frequently for one or two minutes. Add the rest of the ingredients listed, and cook over moderate heat 1 hour uncovered. Reduce heat to a slow simmer and continue cooking, covered, for 1 hour longer. Test beans to make certain they are tender. Now the pot of Cholent is ready to be placed in the ovenette over a very low heat for overnight baking. By placing an asbestos disk over the burner, a well-covered pot containing the Cholent will serve admirably. Make certain that the flame or other heat (like electricity)

does not go out at any time. The moisture formed under the lid is usually sufficient for long cooking, but boiling water may be added if needed.
Serves 6.

CHICKEN SOUP (Basic Recipe)

Fowl that has had the fatty portions removed is best for soup. Sections of chicken should include the gizzard, heart, neck and feet. A 4½- to 5-pound fowl will make 8 to 10 servings of soup. After preparing chicken parts for cooking, add the following:

1 large onion	1 bay leaf
1 large carrot diced, sliced or strips	6 peppercorns, optional
2 stalks celery including leaves	boiled water (1 quart per pound of chicken)

Cook slowly after bringing to a quick boil. Skim carefully. Add vegetables after 30 minutes of simmering. Cooking time depends on tenderness of fowl.

Strain soup while hot just before serving.

Pressure Cooker Method: Cook all ingredients listed 25 to 30 minutes under 15 pounds pressure or as directed in the booklet accompanying your particular type of pressure cooker.

Specially rich clear chicken soup is commonly called *Gilderne Yoich* and is served as a "must" at wedding anniversaries, especially the 25th and 50th.

HOMEMADE NOODLE DOUGH (Basic Recipe)

2 cups sifted flour (approximately)	2 eggs
	2 or 3 teaspoons cold water

Sift flour into mixing bowl or on kneading board. Make a well in the center. Add eggs and combine with a fork, adding spoonfuls of water as necessary to form a ball of dough that is compact but not hard. Knead dough until as smooth and elastic as possible. Roll out on a lightly floured board. Use the rolling pin from the outer edges toward the center, turning the board as necessary in order to achieve easier rolling. When dough is rolled *evenly thin* through the whole round, let stand 10 to 20 minutes in order to dry so that it will not stick together when rolled up. Roll up lightly. Use a sharp knife to cut fine. Shake to loosen and spread noodles on lightly floured cloth. Let dry at room temperature. Store in jars when dried. *Do not try* to make noodle dough in damp weather, especially if you are a novice at it.

SHABBOS KUGEL

8 ounces broad noodles	2 tablespoons chopped *greben*
2 eggs	(cracklings)
3 tablespoons sugar	¼ teaspoon cinnamon
3 tablespoons dry crumbs	1 tablespoon lemon juice
½ teaspoon salt	½ teaspoon grated lemon rind
4 tablespoons schmaltz, melted,	½ cup seedless or seeded raisins
or vegetable shortening	¼ cup chopped almonds

Cook noodles in boiling salted water as per directions on package. When tender, drain and rinse with hot running water. Drain well. Beat eggs, adding sugar gradually till combined. Stir in drained noodles and add dry crumbs, salt, schmaltz, and *greben,* cinnamon, lemon juice and grated rind. Turn half the mixture into a well-greased pudding dish, preferably the one in which the schmaltz has been heated. Add the raisins and almonds and top with remaining noodle mixture. Bake 45 minutes at 400° or till nicely browned on top. Serve with Lemon Sauce, stewed fresh or dried fruit, canned applesauce or cranberry sauce.

May be reheated over asbestos-covered gas or electric burner at low heat, in a well-covered container such as a muffin warmer or a potato baker.

Serves 6 to 8.

Variation: UPSIDE-DOWN PINEAPPLE-NOODLE KUGEL is made by substituting sliced canned pineapple, well drained and dipped in crumbs, for the raisins and almonds. Heat the shortening used in the pudding dish or a 10-inch ring mold. After greasing sides well and pouring melted shortening into the mixture, pack ¾ cup dark brown sugar into bottom of pan. Arrange sliced pineapple over sugar, place a maraschino or nut in the center of each slice and turn in the prepared noodle mixture. Press in well with bowl of mixing spoon. Sprinkle with dry crumbs and bake. Unmold while hot.

GRATED VEGETABLE KUGEL

1 cup each grated raw potato, sweet potato, unpared apple and raw carrot	1 teaspoon each cinnamon, nutmeg or allspice
1 cup dark brown sugar	1 teaspoon salt
1 cup sifted flour	½ cup each raisins and nuts
1 teaspoon baking soda	⅔ cup hot melted vegetable shortening

Pack the grated raw vegetables for accurate measuring. Combine with sugar. Sift together flour, baking soda, spices and salt. Add raisins and nuts, chopped, to half the dry mixture and shake well to coat each raisin and bit of nut. Stir in the prepared vegetable and sugar mixture till combined, then stir in remaining sifted dry ingredients. Add the hot melted shortening, stirring well, and turn into a greased casserole or pudding dish. Cover and bake 1 hour at 375°. Remove cover and continue baking 15 to 20 minutes or till nicely browned on top. Serve plain, hot or cold. Or top with any fruit sauce or stewed dried fruits.

Serves 6 to 8.

OVEN-BROILED CHICKEN

Allow one half of a small spring chicken or one quarter section of the larger ones per portion.

After singeing and preparing the chickens for cooking, pat dry with paper towels and dust lightly with seasoned flour or fine crumbs. By shaking the cut portions in a paper bag containing a mixture of flour or crumbs, white pepper and paprika or garlic salt, excellent results are achieved quickly.

Place the chicken skin side down on the broiler rack about 3 inches from oven flame and broil 10 minutes before turning to broil the outer parts till nicely browned—approximately 15 minutes. A moderate flame is best for the whole process.

Electric broiler method is strongly recommended for tenderness in less time.

Infra red rotisserie method is the latest approved broiling procedure, if you are fortunate enough to own one of these kitchen miracles.

Broiled spring chicken may be served cold, if desired. Cutting the meat away from bones, combining it with diced celery, green pepper and hard-cooked eggs, with enough mayonnaise dressing to suite the taste, is the best way of serving it on days when cooking is forbidden or inconvenient. Allow one cupful of Chicken Salad per serving.

CHICKEN FRICASSEE

5 pound chicken (fowl)	1 medium onion, diced
4 tablespoons flour	1 medium carrot, diced
¼ teaspoon paprika	1 stalk celery, finely cut
a dash of pepper	garlic powder or minced garlic to
4 tablespoons rendered fat	taste, optional
(schmaltz)	water to cover

Section the chicken and remove fat and thick skin. Cut up fat and skin and render for schmaltz. Dredge chicken portions in seasoned flour and sear in the hot fat till lightly browned on all sides. Turn frequently to prevent scorching. Add diced vegetables and garlic for additional seasoning. Cover with water and simmer 2 hours in a partially covered

pot, or till tender. Lift out chicken sections and put gravy through a
strainer. The vegetables may be mashed and added for thickening, or
make an *einbren* by browning 2 tablespoons flour in 2 tablespoons
schmaltz and adding some of the gravy, stirring till free from lumps.
Return chicken to gravy and reheat. Easy to reheat in a covered frying
pan over the pilot light, allowing plenty of time to heat through. Garnish
with minced parsley.

Serves 6 to 8.

STEWED CHICKEN WITH LIMAS

5 to 6 pound stewing chicken, sectioned	1 pound lima beans, soaked overnight
1 large onion, diced	1 cup water or soup stock
1 stalk celery, cut fine	salt to taste when tender
1 carrot, grated	¼ cup honey

Combine the serving portions of chicken, onion, celery, carrot, lima
beans and water in a heavy aluminum pot and bring to a boil quickly.
Cover and cook over low heat, allowing 20 minutes per pound. Test for
tenderness of chicken and lima beans before salting to taste and adding
honey. Cover and cook 30 minutes longer over moderate heat. Can be
reheated over low heat on top of stove.

Serves 8.

ROAST DUCK SECTIONS WITH ORANGE

1 medium-size duckling, 4½ to 5 pounds, sectioned	3 large oranges, sliced without peeling
2 tablespoons flour	juice of 1 lemon
a dash of salt and white pepper (or paprika)	1 clove garlic (optional)

Sprinkle each section of duck with flour and seasoning. Arrange in a
glass casserole or other covered baking dish, tucking in all the orange
slices and arranging plenty over the top. Sprinkle generously with lemon
juice. Stick a toothpick in the clove of garlic if you want to use it and
place it on one side of the duck sections. It can be removed before serving.
Bake 1 hour at 350° tightly covered. Uncover and bake 30 to 40 minutes
longer at 375°, or until nicely browned on top. The fruit juices will flavor
the duck to perfection. Serve with the following sauce:

Wine Sauce for Duckling

½ cup boiling water	¼ cup currant jelly
	½ cup sherry (or white wine)

Combine in a sauce pan and bring to a boil. Serve hot.

Serves 4 to 6.

FRUIT-FILLED DUCKLING

1 medium-size duckling (dressed and prepared for stuffing)	2 tart apples, grated
12 to 18 large pitted prunes, soaked overnight	1 cup dry bread crumbs
	1 egg
	2 tablespoons brown sugar
	½ teaspoon salt

Rub the inside of prepared duck with a cut clove of garlic. Combine the ingredients in the order listed. Fill the duck and sew up or fasten with metal skewers to keep the filling in. Dust duck on all sides with flour. Roast, breast side down, in an open roasting pan 1 hour at 375°. Pour off excess fat and return to oven for 20 to 25 minutes or until nicely browned on under side. This stuffed duckling may be served hot or cold.

Serves 4 to 6.

FRUITED DRESSING FOR DUCK OR GOOSE

3 cups dry bread crumbs (Challah crumbs are best)	½ cup each chopped raisins (seedless kind), chopped walnuts or almonds, canned crushed pineapple, drained
1 teaspoon salt	½ cup orange juice, pulp included
1 cup chopped tart apples	2 tablespoons brown sugar

Combine well and let stand half an hour before using. If any stuffing is left over, make balls of it and place around the roasting duck or goose in the pan as soon as top begins to brown, allowing about 30 minutes for the stuffing balls to brown nicely. Be sure to baste the top of duck or goose with some of the fruit juice during the baking process to insure that fruited taste and glazed look. Allow 35 minutes per pound for a goose not over 10 pounds, and 40 minutes for duck. Roast at 325° till nicely browned.

Double amount of crumbs for 8 to 10 pound turkey.

Thanks to poultry raisers who have developed a special breed of turkeys, this traditional American bird is now heavy-breasted and meated in all parts. It lends itself admirably for Sabbath and holiday main dishes and can be served cold, sliced, on days when cooking is forbidden. It can be purchased, quick-frozen, in kosher meat markets in almost all sections of the country. The bird associated with Thanksgiving Day has taken its place with other poultry. Here are some suggestions for preparing it.

ROAST TURKEY WITH DRESSING

Rub inside of prepared fresh or thawed quick-frozen turkey with a cut clove of garlic or dust with garlic salt, while preparing one of the dressings, as follows:

Prune Dressing

½ pound large prunes, soaked
and pitted
4 tablespoons schmaltz or vegetable shortening
1 onion, finely diced
8 to 10 slices of Challah, diced
and toasted

¼ teaspoon cinnamon, optional
1 teaspoon grated lemon or
orange rind
3 tablespoons sugar
1 cup hot fruit juice of any kind

Prunes soaked overnight in cold water to cover are easily pitted and
cut into halves or quarters. Heat the fat in a large frying pan and sauté
diced onion till light brown. Add the croutons (toasted bread), stirring
3 to 5 minutes over moderate heat. Turn into a mixing bowl, add cut up
prunes, cinnamon, grated rind, sugar and hot fruit juice, stirring lightly
with two forks till liquid is absorbed. Let cool before filling cavity of the
bird and sew up skin or secure with small metal skewers. Roast in an open
pan at 300°, allowing 25 minutes per pound, or till browned.

This amount of dressing is sufficient for an 8 to 10 pound turkey.

Bread Crumb and Giblet Dressing

5 to 6 cups dry bread crumbs
(white, whole wheat or rye)
cooked and chopped gizzard
3 tablespoons schmaltz or other
shortening
1 large onion, diced

1 teaspoon celery salt or ¼ cup
diced celery
⅛ teaspoon mixed herb poultry
seasoning
2 eggs
1 cup soup stock (from cooked
giblets, neck, etc.)

Place bread crumbs in a shallow baking pan in a 400° oven for a few
minutes to dry thoroughly, or slip under broiler flame for a few seconds
till lightly browned. Turn into a mixing bowl till cool. Cut the cooked
gizzard or put through coarse blade of food chopper. Melt the schmaltz
in a frying pan and lightly brown the diced onion and prepared gizzard
over moderate heat. Combine with the toasted crumbs, adding seasonings,
eggs and soup stock. Stir lightly and use as stuffing for turkey, goose,
ducks or chickens. Sufficient for two 5 to 6 pound chickens, one medium-
size goose or an 8 to 10 pound turkey.

Variation: Substitute 1 cup sliced, roasted chestnuts for the prunes
or chopped giblets in above dressings.

Rice and Raisin Dressing

3 cups parboiled long grain or brown rice, drained
2 cups dry bread or cracker crumbs
½ cup seedless raisins coated with flour
3 eggs

2 tablespoons sugar
1 teaspoon salt
1 cup diced onions browned in
4 tablespoons schmaltz or oil
¼ teaspoon poultry seasoning, optional
¼ teaspoon cinnamon, optional

Combine in the order listed. Excellent as dressing for chicken, duck, goose or turkey.

RICE-FILLED LAMB BREAST (Sephardic Recipe)

1 breast of lamb (with pocket cut for stuffing)
¾ cup brown rice (or converted rice), parboiled 20 minutes, drained
½ teaspoon salt

3 tablespoons crushed pine nuts (peanuts or pecans)
2 tablespoons minced parsley
4 tablespoons of salad oil (olive oil preferred)
2 cups boiling water

Trim off some of the bits of fat from the meat and cut fine or chop. Combine with rice, salt, nuts, and parsley and use as stuffing. Close the opening with toothpicks or metal skewers. Brown lightly on all sides in some of the oil. Dust lightly with flour and roast in an open pan at 350°, adding a half cup of boiling water at a time as needed during the roasting process. The meat should not be permitted to become dry. Be sure to use the remaining oil with the hot water after greasing the pan well. Serve with any green vegetable, tomato sauce or just plain.
Serves 6.

ROAST SHOULDER OF LAMB

1 average-weight lamb shoulder, bone in
garlic salt or cut clove of garlic
2 tablespoons flour
¼ teaspoon paprika, optional
¼ teaspoon pepper, optional

3 tablespoons melted shortening or schmaltz
2 large onions, thinly sliced
2 carrots, thinly sliced
1 stalk celery, optional

Trim away fat from meat and dust with garlic salt or rub with garlic on all sides. Roll in flour and sprinkle with paprika and pepper if used. Spread the melted fat in bottom of an open roasting pan and spread sliced onions, carrots and celery evenly before placing the lamb shoulder in. Roast in a preheated oven at 325°, allowing 25 to 30 minutes per pound of meat, till lightly browned on top.
Serves 6 or more.

VEAL BREAST, CHOPPED BEEF FILLING

1 average-size veal breast
1 pound chopped beef
1 onion, grated
1 carrot, grated
2 eggs
¼ cup rice, parboiled and drained
¼ teaspoon paprika, optional
¼ teaspoon poultry seasoning, optional

4 tablespoons dry bread or cracker crumbs
2 tablespoons cold water or soup stock
flour for dusting meat
2 tablespoons oil or melted shortening of any kind

Cut a pocket in the veal breast for the filling. Combine the chopped beef, grated onion and carrot, eggs, drained rice, mixing thoroughly. Add seasonings, crumbs and liquid and combine by mixing with a fork. Fill the veal breast, patting it to remove air pockets inside. Dust with flour, top and bottom, and roast in a well-greased open baking pan, allowing 25 to 30 minutes of combined meat weight. When nicely browned on top, turn to brown underside. Can be reheated on top of stove in a well-covered frying pan over low heat. If sliced, grease the frying pan in which it is to be reheated.

Serves 6 to 8.

RISI-BISI (Rice and Peas)

1 cup long-grain converted rice
3 tablespoons shortening
1 large onion, diced
1 green pepper, diced, optional
1 tablespoon salt

6 cups boiling water or soup stock
1½ cups fresh, frozen, or canned peas

Wash and drain the rice. Melt shortening in a heavy frying pan and sauté onion and green pepper till light brown. Add the rice and stir for 1 minute till well mixed with the browned onion and pepper. Add salt and boiling water gradually, then cover and cook over low heat for 25 minutes or till the rice is tender and the liquid almost completely absorbed. Add the fresh peas and cook 15 minutes longer. If quick-frozen or canned peas are used, cook under cover 3 minutes. Remove cover and slip under broiler flame to brown lightly on top before serving. Or turn into a casserole for reheating in moderate oven.

Serves 6.

GREEN BEANS AND ALMONDS

1 pound fresh or quick-frozen green beans
¼ cup hot water or soup stock

¼ cup slivered blanched almonds
1 teaspoon lemon juice
1 teaspoon brown sugar

If fresh beans are used, cut diagonally or lengthwise and cook in slightly salted cold water 8 to 10 minutes or till tender enough to pierce with a fork. If frozen beans are used, drop into hot water or soup stock, cover and cook 4 to 5 minutes. Canned beans require only heating over moderate flame. Add almonds, lemon juice and brown sugar and cook 1 minute before serving.

Wax beans may be substituted for the green beans.

Serves 6.

UNCOOKED NIPPY CRANBERRY RELISH

3 cups fresh cranberries (about 1 pound)
¾ cup sugar
½ cup seeded raisins

2 whole oranges, seedless or seeds removed
1 large apple, pared and cored
¾ teaspoon ground ginger or 3 tablespoons candied ginger root

Pick over cranberries, removing stems and points. Wash and drain well. Cover with sugar and let stand 15 minutes. Put raisins and cut oranges and apples through the medium blade of your food chopper, or chop in a wooden bowl. Add sweetened cranberries and ground ginger or finely cut ginger root, put through food chopper for finer consistency. Let stand in refrigerator at least an hour before serving. Honey may be substituted for sugar or added if required for sweeter relish.

BEET SALAD

2 cups diced cooked beets
4 tablespoons prepared horse-radish

2 tablespoons salad oil
salt and pepper to taste

Combine horseradish, oil and seasoning. Add to beets. Serve on lettuce. Serves 4.

PICKLED BEET RELISH

Chop pickled beets. Add 1 tablespoon prepared horseradish to each cupful. Add lemon juice and brown sugar to taste. Let stand a half hour before serving.

RAW CARROT SALAD (Basic Recipe)

2 cups shredded raw carrot, tightly packed
1 tablespoon minced parsley
2 tablespoons coarsely ground walnuts or almonds

1 teaspoon grated orange rind
2 tablespoons orange juice
2 tablespoons mayonnaise dressing
lettuce

Combine in the order listed and serve in lettuce cups or on shredded lettuce.

Serves 6.

CARROT AND PINEAPPLE RING

2 packages lemon-flavored gelatin
2 cups boiling hot water
1 cup syrup from canned pineapple
1 teaspoon grated lemon rind
1 tablespoon lemon juice

¼ cup slivered almonds
2 cups grated carrot (tightly packed)
1 cup drained, crushed canned pineapple
¼ cup chopped green pepper, optional

Dissolve the gelatin in hot water in a large bowl. Chill 1 hour in the refrigerator. Stir in remaining listed ingredients in the order named and turn into a lightly greased 9-inch ring mold. Chill till firm before unmolding on a large serving plate, and garnish with shredded salad greens such as lettuce, chicory, etc. Green pepper strips and/or raw carrot curls make an attractive garnish.

Serves 6 to 8.

A good standby for holiday entertaining is the traditional Lekach, or Honey Cake. There are several variations of this tasty morsel—even a variety that is made without benefit of shortening, a boon to those who must eliminate or cut down on fat intake in their daily diet. Here are two varieties that will meet with your needs—with and without shortening.

LEKACH (Honey Cake)

1 cup vegetable shortening
1 cup honey
1 cup dark brown sugar (tightly packed)
3 eggs
1 cup very strong black coffee, hot

2 teaspoons baking powder
1 teaspoon baking soda
3½ cups sifted all-purpose flour
¼ teaspoon salt
¼ teaspoon ground ginger
¾ cup chopped nuts (any one or several kinds)

Cream shortening, honey and sugar, then add one egg at a time while continuing to beat the mixture till smooth. Combine hot coffee, baking powder and baking soda in a pitcher to prevent bubbling over. Add this gradually and alternately with the sifted flour, salt and ginger, to the creamed mixture, stirring well till free of lumps. Dust the chopped nuts with a little flour and fold in last. Turn the batter into two greased and waxpaper- or aluminum-lined loaf pans, 9 x 4 x 3½, filling two-thirds full. Bake 1 hour at 325°. Test by inserting a wooden toothpick in center of cakes. If the toothpick comes out dry, the cakes are done. Remove from oven and let cool over a wire rack. Remove from pans and slice when cold.

FAT-FREE HONEY CAKE

1 pound honey
2 teaspoons baking soda
1 cup strong black coffee, hot
3 eggs

1 cup sugar
3 cups all-purpose flour
1 teaspoon each cinnamon, all-
    spice and ginger

Heat the honey in a large saucepan till it begins to bubble, then stir in the baking soda. The mixture will fizz up, so be sure to stir it down. Stir in the hot coffee and remove from heat till lukewarm, during which time prepare the other ingredients. Beat eggs till creamy, adding sugar a little at a time, till well combined, light and thick. Sift together the flour, spices—two or three times. Combine the creamed mixture with the cool honey and coffee mixture, then add to the dry ingredients gradually, a little at a time while stirring till smooth.

Line a 14 x 9-inch baking pan with aluminum foil or waxpaper and turn in the cake batter. Bake at 300° for 50 to 55 minutes or till set. Test by inserting a wooden toothpick in the center of cake. If it comes out dry and the edges stand away from sides of pan, remove from oven and let cool in the pan placed over a wire rack away from draughts. Cut into 1½- or 2-inch squares or into diagonal cuts when ready to serve. This cake keeps well if covered with aluminum foil. Store in cake box or in refrigerator.

LEKACH DE LUXE

6 eggs or 4 eggs plus ½ cup
    strong coffee
1 cup sugar
1 cup honey, warmed
2 tablespoons salad oil or melted
    shortening
3½ cups sifted flour
1½ teaspoons baking powder
1 teaspoon baking soda

½ teaspoon salt
1 teaspoon cinnamon
½ teaspoon ginger
¼ teaspoon nutmeg
a dash of cloves (optional)
1 cup chopped seeded raisins and
    walnuts
¼ cup finely cut citron
2 tablespoons brandy

Beat eggs, adding sugar gradually while beating with a rotary beater. When the mixture is light and creamy, stir in the honey and shortening. If using four eggs and coffee, dilute the honey in the hot coffee before combining with the beaten eggs and sugar mixture. Be sure the coffee combination is cooled to lukewarm, however. Sift all dry ingredients together and add the nuts, raisins and citron, stirring until the fruit is well-coated. Stir into the first mixture until well combined and then add the brandy.

Turn into a well-greased, paper-lined rectangular cake pan, 9 x 12. Preheat the oven to 310° and bake 1 hour. Invert over a cake rack until cool before removing from the pan. Remove the paper before cutting into squares or diamond shapes.

Variation: The nuts and fruit may be omitted and sherry substituted for the brandy. Follow the same procedure.

HONEY-ORANGE CAKE

2 cups sifted cake flour
3½ teaspoons baking powder
¾ teaspoon salt
½ cup sugar
½ cup butter or vegetable shortening

⅔ cup honey
2 eggs, separated
½ cup orange juice
¼ teaspoon grated orange rind

Sift together three times flour, baking powder and salt. Cream shortening with sugar until light and fluffy and stir in honey until blended. Add egg yolks to creamy mixture and beat well. Combine alternately flour mixture with orange juice and grated rind, beating after each addition until smooth. Beat egg whites stiff but not dry, and fold in. Bake in two well-greased 9-inch layer cake pans 30 to 35 minutes at 350°. Put together when cold with the following frosting:

Boiled Honey Frosting and Filling

1½ cups honey
⅛ teaspoon salt

1 egg white
½ teaspoon vanilla

Cook honey and salt to 238° or until a drop makes a soft ball in cold water. Beat egg white in a bowl and pour the syrup in gradually, beating until all the syrup has been added and the mixture will hold a peak. Add vanilla and beat a few strokes. Spread between layers and on top of cake.

SPONGE CAKE

6 eggs, separated
1 tablespoon lemon juice

1 cup sugar
1 cup flour, sifted

Beat egg whites stiff but not dry; then beat in half the cup of sugar a little at a time while beating with spoon or electric beater. Beat egg yolks and lemon juice till thick and fold into the egg whites mixture as lightly as possible. Combine sifted flour with remaining sugar and sift into the batter, scraping down the sides of bowl with a rubber spatula while mixing gradually till combined into a smooth mixture. Turn into an ungreased tube pan and bake 35 minutes at 375° or till light pressure of the index finger leaves no depression. Invert the pan with baked cake over a wire cake rack or hang on the neck of a strong bottle so that air circulates till cake has cooled. Remove from pan when cold. Serve plain or with fruit.

LOAF SPONGE CAKE

6 eggs, separated	1¼ cups sifted sugar
⅛ teaspoon salt	1½ tablespoons lemon juice
½ teaspoon cream of tartar	1¼ cups cake flour, sifted

Beat egg whites with salt till foamy. Add cream of tartar and beat till stiff before adding sugar gradually, beating till the mixture holds a peak. Beat egg yolks lightly, add lemon juice and stir well. Fold in the beaten whites, then the flour, gradually, till well blended. Pour into an ungreased 10 x 5 x 3-inch loaf pan and bake 1 hour and 10 minutes at 300° or till pressure of the index finger leaves no depression in center of cake. Invert on a wire rack to cool before removing from pan.

SHTRUDEL

Shtrudel is the pastry that is as Jewish as pie is American. And there are many variations of both these pastries, depending on locality and family custom. For instance, Shtrudel made by Austrian or Hungarian cooks is made of a paper-thin stretched dough with fillings of apple, prune butter, cheese and raisins. Rumanians also pride themselves on the paper-thin stretched Shtrudel dough wrapped around chopped nuts, thinly sliced apples, etc. Polish and Russian cooks use a thinly rolled dough filled with finely chopped cabbage, chopped meat or chicken, kasha (buckwheat groats), all seasoned superbly, and baked to a luscious golden brown in long rolls, then cut into diagonal slices 1¼ to 2 inches wide and browned on the cut sides. Of course sweet fillings are popular!

Shtrudel of the fruit or nut and raisin filled variety is generally "on tap" for holidays wherever Jews are found. And what a toothsome pastry a well-made Shtrudel can be! It may take some practice for the novice to achieve a stretched dough Shtrudel, filled and baked to a delicious crispness. But it is certainly worth the effort.

STRETCHED SHTRUDEL DOUGH

2 cups flour (sifted several times)	1 egg
1 tablespoon salad oil or melted vegetable shortening	½ cup lukewarm water (approximately)
	⅛ teaspoon salt

Use a deep mixing bowl. Into the sifted flour stir the mixture of oil, slightly beaten egg, water and salt, working from the center until a ball of dough is formed. Turn out on a lightly floured kneading board and work the dough till smooth and elastic to the touch. Warm the mixing bowl and turn it over to cover the mound of dough. Let stand while preparing the filling mixture—approximately 30 minutes. Roll out with rolling pin as thin as possible. Transfer the sheet of dough to a lightly floured cloth, and with the back of hand and deft use of fingers stretch the dough to tissue paper thinness. Brush the dough with a little melted shortening or salad oil and work the fingers under dough from the center to the outer edges, stretching the dough evenly. Cut away any thick edges that remain. Yes, it takes time and patience, but it is all a matter of experience to achieve worthwhile results.

The dough is ready for filling and rolling. Drizzle a little melted shortening or oil over the whole surface and sprinkle generously with a mixture of sugar and cinnamon if the filling is to be a sweet one. Spread the thinly sliced apples evenly, sprinkle with lemon juice, grated rind of orange or lemon, sugar and fine cracker or dry bread crumbs to absorb the moisture. Drizzle more shortening over all and roll up by gently lifting the cloth at one side and giving the dough a start with a pat or two. By lifting the cloth with both hands, the rolling-up process takes care of itself. Pat the rolled, filled dough gently with the fingers. Cut away edges at both ends, then cut into lengths to fit the baking pan or cookie sheet. Be sure to grease the bottom of the pan before placing the rolls at least 2 inches apart lengthwise. Bake at 375° 35 to 45 minutes or until nicely browned. Brushing the top with melted shortening adds crispness but is not essential. When baked, permit to cool in the pan before cutting into desired sections. Return cut pieces to baking pan and bake 5 minutes longer to brown the cut sides.

SHTRUDEL FILLINGS

Apple

8 cups thinly sliced tart apples
1 cup chopped seedless or seeded raisins
¾ cup sugar
3 tablespoons dry bread or cracker crumbs

½ teaspoon cinnamon
⅛ teaspoon nutmeg
½ teaspoon grated lemon or orange rind, optional
4 tablespoons melted shortening or salad oil

Cherry

3 cups well drained canned sour cherries
1 cup crushed dry cereal (corn or rice flakes)

¾ cup sugar
¼ cup shredded coconut, optional

Cheese

½ pound sieved dry pot cheese
½ pound cream cheese
2 eggs
½ cup sugar

¼ cup dry crumbs (cookies, crackers or bread)
1 tablespoon grated lemon rind
½ cup currant or seedless raisins, optional

Kasha Groats

2 cups cooked buckwheat groats
1 onion, diced fine
4 tablespoons schmaltz

½ cup chopped *greben* (cracklings)
2 eggs

Liver

1 pound beef, calves' or chicken livers, broiled and chopped
1 onion, diced fine

4 tablespoons schmaltz or olive oil
¼ cup crushed dry cereal flakes
1 teaspoon salt
⅛ teaspoon pepper, optional

Raisins and Almonds

1½ cups seeded raisins, chopped
¼ pound blanched almonds, ground or chopped fine
4 hard cooked egg yolks

½ cup brown sugar
1 tablespoon grated lemon rind
4 tablespoons dry crumbs or matzo meal

Note: Fruit fillings and raisins and almond combination should be cooked in top of double boiler over hot water for 15 to 20 minutes or till very soft in order to insure tender fillings.

ONEG SHABBAT

These Hebrew words mean "Sabbath joy," or joy in the Sabbath. The day of rest was decreed a holiday for man to enjoy in every way, in accordance with his fondest desires, his noblest interests.

Inviting a stranger in town to partake of the Sabbath meal after services is a time-honored custom. During war periods, men in service are the guests. Hospitality to the "stranger within thy gates" is made real, literally and figuratively.

This traditional custom has been extended currently to include the entire Synagogue congregation. After Friday evening services in Temples and Synagogues, a social hour in the Assembly Hall is enjoyed by all in attendance. Some important topic of the day is brought up for informal discussion; a noteworthy book or play may be the subject introduced by the rabbi or some lay leader.

The hospitality committee serves food, always a stimulant to conversation. And it is for such hostesses that suggestions for refreshments easily prepared and served are offered in the following pages. It is well to remember that where the services of a caterer are not employed, refreshments must be kept simple. Cookies and small cakes have become standard *kibbet,* for these can be eaten out of hand. Special consideration has been given the types of sweets that can be baked by committee members in their own home kitchens. Keeping the *Oneg Shabbat* simple adds to the joy of the Sabbath.

COOKIES (Basic Recipe)

1 cup butter or margarine	⅛ teaspoon salt (if unsalted butter is used)
1 cup sugar	
2 eggs	1 teaspoon vanilla extract
	2½ cups sifted all-purpose flour

Cream butter or margarine and sugar till fluffy. Add one egg at a time, creaming well after each addition. Add salt (if used) and vanilla, then stir in the sifted flour, a little at a time till well combined into a ball of dough. Wrap in aluminum foil or waxpaper; chill over night. When ready to bake, roll out part of the dough to ⅛-inch thickness between two squares of waxpaper or on a lightly floured board. Cut into desired shapes and place on an ungreased cookie sheet. Decorate the cookies as desired. Roll out the next piece of dough and do likewise. Bake at 350° for 8 to 10 minutes or till lightly browned. Let cool before removing to the cookie jar for storing.

Yields approximately 60.

DECORATIVE IDEAS FOR COOKIES

Cut cookie dough with a fluted cutter to form trees and decorate with green or red colored sugar or sprinkles.

Cut into six-pointed stars and decorate with six almond halves, points meeting at center. Press nuts in lightly.

Brush each cookie, in whatever shape desired, with beaten egg white, then sprinkle with chopped nuts. Press nuts down lightly with the forefinger before baking.

Cut dough into crescent shapes, brush with diluted egg yolk or evaporated milk, sprinkle with colored sugar or poppy seeds.

Use tiny strips of candied cherries, citron, pineapple, etc., for decorating any shape cookie.

BLACK WALNUT MACAROONS

4 egg whites
¼ teaspoon salt
1 teaspoon vanilla

½ pound powdered sugar
1 teaspoon cake flour
1½ tablespoons fine bread crumbs
1 cup chopped black walnuts

Beat egg whites with salt at room temperature till stiff but not dry. Add the vanilla a few drops at a time while beating, then fold in the sugar mixed with flour, bread crumbs and chopped nuts. Drop the mixture on heavy waxpaper-lined cookie sheet, allowing at least 2 inches between drops. A teaspoon half filled is a good measure for these macaroons. Bake at 325° for 40 minutes.

Yields approximately 3 dozen.

DATE DROPS

1 cup finely cut or chopped dates
3 cups graham cracker crumbs

½ teaspoon cinnamon
1 can sweetened condensed milk

Blend ingredients in the order listed. Drop from the tip of a teaspoon on a buttered cookie sheet. Bake 15 minutes at 375° or till nicely browned.

Yields approximately 36 drops.

CHOCOLATE COOKIES

3 egg whites
1 cup confectioners' sugar
½ cup graham cracker crumbs
½ cup coarsely ground pecans or almonds

1 teaspoon vanilla
6 ounces semi-sweet chocolate, melted
1 tablespoon butter or substitute

Beat egg whites stiff but not dry. Fold in the sugar gradually till well combined. Fold in the cracker crumbs, nuts, flavoring, then the melted chocolate. Drop the mixture from the tip of a teaspoon onto a well-buttered sheet, leaving an inch of space between drops each way. Bake 12 minutes at 325°. Let cool on the pan before removing.

Yields approximately 3 dozen.

FESTIVAL COOKIES

1 cup honey
1 cup sugar
2 tablespoons orange juice
1 ounce each candied orange and
  lemon peel
1 ounce citron
2 cups blanched almonds
2 cups sifted all-purpose flour

½ teaspoon salt
¼ teaspoon each cinnamon, nutmeg, allspice
2 tablespoons vegetable shortening
confectioners' sugar frosting for
  decoration
chopped almonds, grated orange
  rind and sugar or colored
  sprinkles for trimming

Heat honey and add sugar and orange juice. Chop candied peel and citron very fine or put through food chopper, using medium blade. Put almonds through food chopper or chop very fine with the candied peel. Combine with the honey mixture and add the dry ingredients that have been sifted together. Mix the two combinations thoroughly and cover. Chill for 8 days, then roll very thin on a lightly floured board. Cut into various shapes and bake on a well-greased cookie sheet 10 to 12 minutes at 325°. Let cool before spreading with frosting and decorating as desired. Store these cookies in a tightly covered cookie jar or tin container before using. They are best when aged about 2 weeks before serving.
Yields approximately 5 dozen.

GINGER WAFERS

1 cup butter or substitute
2 cups dark brown sugar
3 cups cake flour

¼ teaspoon salt
1 cup milk
1 teaspoon ground ginger
1 cup chopped pecans

Cream butter and sugar. Add alternately the flour mixed with salt and the milk till well combined. Add the ginger and beat till absorbed. Spread this mixture very thinly on two buttered and flour-dusted cookie sheets and sprinkle with chopped nuts. Bake 12 minutes at 325° or till a toothpick test proves the dough baked through but not dry. Cut into 2-inch squares and roll to form cornucopias while hot. They will hold their shape if cooled slowly away from draughts.
Yields 6 to 7 dozen, depending on thickness of the layers.

NEVER-FAIL COOKIES

½ cup butter or substitute
⅔ cup sugar
1 egg yolk
1½ cups sifted flour

½ teaspoon salt
1 teaspoon baking powder
1 tablespoon sherry or fruit juice
1 teaspoon vanilla or ¼ teaspoon
  almond extract

Soften the shortening at room temperature and stir in sugar till well combined. Add the other ingredients in the order listed, blending with a pastry blender or fork to form a ball of dough. Divide into four parts and form into 1-inch-thick rolls. Cut each roll into even pieces, making 60 small parts. Roll each into a round ball and press a raisin, piece of nut, bit of candied fruit or citron into the centers. Bake at 325° on a greased cookie sheet 7 minutes or till nicely browned. Remove from pan with a spatula. Store, when cold, in a covered container.

Yields 5 dozen.

REFRIGERATOR NUT COOKIES

1 cup butter	½ teaspoon salt
½ cup sugar	6 drops almond extract
3 cups sifted flour	½ cup coarsely chopped nuts (walnuts, Brazil nuts or pecans)

Cream butter. Add sugar gradually while beating until fluffy, then work in remaining ingredients till well combined. Shape into two rolls 1½ inches in diameter. Wrap in waxed paper or aluminum foil and chill 2 hours in refrigerator. Unwrap and slice into ⅛-inch thick rounds. Arrange on ungreased cookie sheets and bake 10 to 12 minutes at 350°.

Yields 12 dozen.

REFRIGERATOR NUT-DATE COOKIES

½ cup vegetable shortening	½ teaspoon salt
1 cup brown sugar, firmly packed	¼ teaspoon baking soda
½ teaspoon vanilla	½ cup chopped dates
1 egg	½ cup chopped nuts (walnuts,
1¾ cups sifted all-purpose flour	hazelnuts, or pecans)

Cream shortening and add sugar, flavoring and egg. Beat till light. Sift together dry ingredients and reserve about ¼ cup in which dates and nuts should be rolled. Stir in the dry mixture gradually, mixing well after each addition. Stir in floured dates and nuts and shape dough into a 2-inch thick roll. Wrap in waxpaper or aluminum foil and chill overnight. Unwrap and slice as thin as desired. Arrange cookies on a greased cookie sheet and bake 8 to 10 minutes at 375°.

Yields 3 dozen.

Variation: Omit dates. Make Raisin-Nut Cookies by chopping ½ cup seeded raisins with ½ cup mixed nuts and add as in basic recipe.

FRUIT-FILLED COOKIES

¾ cup vegetable shortening
1 cup sugar
½ teaspoon vanilla
2 eggs
3½ cups sifted cake flour

3 teaspoons baking powder
1 teaspoon salt
⅓ cup milk or water
   apricot or other colorful preserves
36 whole blanched almonds

Cream shortening, add sugar, flavoring and eggs, one at a time, beating after each addition till well blended and light. Sift together dry ingredients and add alternately with liquid till well combined. Roll out to ⅛-inch thickness on a lightly floured board. Divide in half. Cut one portion with a 2-inch scalloped cookie cutter, round or diamond-shaped. Cut the other portion with a small round cutter. Place the scalloped-edge cookies on a well-greased cookie sheet and spread with preserves. Place a small round cookie on top and a dot of preserves in the center. Place an almond on each cookie and bake 10 minutes at 400° or till lightly browned.

Yields approximately 3 dozen.

HAZELNUT COOKIES (also called Hazelnut Rings)

1½ cups sugar
¾ cup softened vegetable shortening
1 cup finely ground hazelnuts

2 cups sifted all-purpose flour
½ teaspoon salt
1 teaspoon vanilla
2 egg whites, beaten stiff

Cream 1 cup sugar with the shortening till smooth and combine with the finely ground nuts. Sift flour and salt together and return to sifter for sifting a small amount into the creamed mixture; stir till blended before sifting in the next portion and until the mixture is smooth. Stir in the flavoring as lightly as possible and turn out the dough on a lightly floured board. Cover with heavy waxpaper and roll out to ½-inch thickness. Use a doughnut cutter to make the rings and lift from the board to a greased and lightly floured cookie sheet. Place the small centers between the rings. By dividing the dough into two or three portions, the rolling and cutting will be facilitated. When all the centers and rings are in place, make a meringue topping by beating a little of the remaining half cup of sugar into the beaten egg whites till absorbed before adding a little more and proceeding to beat till thick enough to spread with the tip of a teaspoon on both rings and center rounds. Bake 12 to 15 minutes at 300° and remove from pan when cool.

Yields 60 rings and 60 rounds.

NUT FINGERS

⅔ cup margarine
6 tablespoons confectioners' sugar
1 teaspoon vanilla
2 cups sifted flour

½ teaspoon almond extract
¼ teaspoon salt
1 cup chopped nuts
powdered sugar

Cream the shortening and add the other ingredients in the order listed, mixing thoroughly into a ball of dough. Roll pieces of dough into ½-inch thick lengths and cut these into 1½- or 2-inch fingers, tapered at the ends. Bake on ungreased cookie sheet 30 minutes at 325° and roll each in the powdered sugar while warm.

Yields 3½ dozen.

SNOWBALLS

1 cup butter or vegetable shortening
¾ cup granulated sugar
2¼ cups sifted pastry flour
¼ teaspoon salt

¼ teaspoon nutmeg
¾ cup finely chopped mixed nuts
1 teaspoon vanilla or ½ teaspoon almond extract
1 cup sifted confectioners' sugar

Cream butter or shortening and sugar and sift together the dry ingredients while continuing to cream the mixture till well combined into a smooth and heavy batter thick enough to form into balls. Add the chopped nuts and a few drops at a time of the flavoring used, continuing to pat the dough on a lightly floured board if more convenient to handle. Pinch off bits of dough and form balls an inch in diameter. Roll these in confectioners' sugar, using a paper bag for about four or five balls at a time and shaking to distribute the sugar coating. Place on an ungreased cookie sheet about 2 inches apart each way. Bake 10 to 12 minutes at 400° or till firm to the touch. If desired, roll again in confectioners' sugar after the snowballs are cool enough to handle.

Yields 48 to 56.

SEED-TOPPED COOKIES

½ cup butter
6 tablespoons sugar
1¾ cups sifted flour
1½ teaspoons baking powder

½ teaspoon salt
¼ cup cold water
1 teaspoon each of poppy seed, caraway seed and sesame seed

Cream butter, add sugar and then sifted-together dry ingredients. Blend well with pastry cutter or fingers, then add water enough to make a stiff ball of dough. Divide into thirds and roll out each portion to ⅛-inch thickness, on a floured board. Sprinkle the seeds on dough, roll lightly to firm the seeds, then cut into desired shapes. Bake 10 minutes at 400°.

Yields 4 to 5 dozen.

KOMISHBRODT (Mandelbrodt)

1 cup sugar
3 eggs
6 tablespoons salad oil
grated rind of 1 lemon
1 teaspoon lemon juice

¼ teaspoon almond extract
2¾ cups flour
4 teaspoons baking powder
¼ teaspoon salt
½ cup coarsely cut blanched almonds (peeling removed)

Beat sugar and eggs until light. Stir in the oil and flavorings. Sift together flour, baking powder and salt. Combine, adding almonds while stirring together to form a ball of dough. Knead on a floured board and form into rolls 1 inch thick and 3 inches wide when flattened. Bake 40 to 45 minutes at 350° or until light brown. Remove to a bread board and slice while warm into half inch wide cuts, slicing diagonally. Place the slices cut side up on a cookie sheet and slip under the broiler flame for quick browning, or return to the top shelf of oven till browned on both sides.

Yields approximately 36 to 40 slices.

ROSH HASHONAH, BEGINNING OF THE YEAR

The month of Tishri is the seventh month of the Hebrew calendar. Traditionally the first day of this month has been called "the first day of creation," and perhaps for that reason the New Year or beginning of the year, Rosh Hashonah, was established on the first and second day of the month.

Another theory is that the planting of the new crop in Palestine or ancient Israel came at that time of the year. The Hebrews were an agricultural people—a very logical explanation for making the beginning of the New Year not the first calendar month but the seventh month, Tishri, the agricultural New Year.

While in our time, in the western world, Rosh Hashonah is celebrated on Tishri 1st and 2nd (except by Reform Temples), in Israel it is only a one-day holiday. It is celebrated with feasting as well as prayer, in keeping with the words of the Prophet Nehemiah, who is said to have introduced the Persian custom of "something sweet" for this holiday. Remember his often quoted phrase: "Eat of the fat and drink the sweet," symbolizing humanity's desire for a year of fullness and prosperity to come for all mankind.

During the Babylonian days of residence, another food custom was incorporated in the foodlore associated with this holiday. For the main course of the feast a whole sheep's head was served, symbolizing in a graphic manner "the head of the year." Another interpretation of this ancient custom is that it commemorates Abraham's sacrifice of a ram in lieu of his son Isaac.

Several more food customs have accumulated about Rosh Hashonah. One is to serve honey and apples to all around the festive board. This beautiful symbol, the bowl of honey and the plate of apple slices, has but one meaning—sweetness for all in the New Year ahead.

Another food custom is to serve a *tzimmes,* especially of carrots, as the main dish. This is a "sweet" combination of carrots, potatoes and meat, cooked with sugar and/or honey to a rich, golden color. While there are a number of variations of Carrot *Tzimmes,* several kinds of combinations have come into that category, as will be noted by the recipes in this section. All, however, are sweet and succulent Rosh Hashonah dishes, time-honored, traditional.

The very word, *tzimmes,* has crept into the vernacular and become a folk expression. For instance, to say that one "makes a tzimmes over" a person or incident is equivalent to "making a fuss over something," happily, of course, a bit of exaggerated praise.

In the following suggested menus for this beautiful festival of Rosh Hashonah when cooking is permitted (except if it fall on Sabbath), we have tried to present as many forms of *tzimmes* and variations as it has been our pleasure to collect from several generations of family and friends. So "eat of the fat and drink of the sweet," and a happy, healthy, socially useful New Year to all!

Suggested Menus for Rosh Hashonah

Menu 1

Broiled Grapefruit Halves
Dish of Carrot Curls, Celery Sticks,
Green Pepper Rings, Olives
Carrot Tzimmes
Pageant Salad
Hot or Cold Beverage
Fat-free Honey Cake

Menu 2

Gefilte Fish
Chicken Soup with Farfel
Prune and Rice Tzimmes
Uncooked Cranberry, Apple and
Nut Relish
Hot or Cold Beverage
Cookies

Menu 3

Sweet-Sour Fish
Chicken Soup with Crackers
Rutabaga Tzimmes
Uncooked Nippy Cranberry Relish
Hot or Cold Beverage
Shtrudel

Menu 4

Fruit Cup
Fresh Caviar (Icre de Carp)
Prune and Potato Tzimmes
Tossed Greens Salad
Cider or Apple Juice
Komishbrodt

Menu 5

Pickled Smelts
Chicken Soup with Noodles
Roast Duck or Goose with
Fruited Dressing
Sliced Tomato Salad
Hot or Cold Beverage
Stangerl

Menu 6

Broiled Fish Patties
Carrot Tzimmes with Knaidle
Sunburst Salad
Hot or Cold Beverage
Tayglach mit Neshomes

BROILED GRAPEFRUIT HALVES

With a sharp pointed paring knife cut into the grapefruit middle section, between stem and blossom ends, making half-inch to three-quarter inch diagonal cuts, forming pointed or scalloped edges of both halves. Be sure to cut to the center of grapefruit, making each cut of equal size. With a twist of both halves, separate and remove seeds. Use a pair of scissors to cut out center. Drizzle with honey before placing under the broiler flame for 2 to 3 minutes or till lightly browned at the peaks.

Garnish with a maraschino cherry, red or green, for color accents. Or place a pitted cooked prune or canned apricot half in center of each grapefruit half. Adds a very festive touch to the holiday table.

PICKLED SMELTS

4 dozen small or medium-size smelts (about 5 pounds)	1 large onion, thinly sliced
flour for dusting (about ½ cup)	1 cup diced celery, leaves included
salt and pepper (1 tablespoon mixed to taste)	1 carrot, thinly sliced
oil or vegetable shortening for frying	6 bay leaves
	12 peppercorns
	2 red-hot peppers
	1½ cups pickling vinegar
	¼ cup brown sugar

Clean the smelts carefully, removing entrails. Wash and wipe dry. Combine flour, salt and pepper mixture. Roll smelts in same till lightly coated. Heat enough oil or shortening in a frying pan to cover the smelts adequately. Fry on one side till nice and brown before turning to brown the other side. Lift out fried smelts and place them in a crock or large glass container, being careful not to break them in the process. Combine the other ingredients listed and bring to a boil. Pour over the fried smelts, cover and let stand till cool before refrigerating. Can be served same day as fried. Will keep well for two weeks.

Serves 24 as appetizer course.

TZIMMES KNAIDLE

1 cup all-purpose flour	½ cup chopped beef suet
½ teaspoon baking powder	1 tablespoon minced parsley (optional)
⅛ teaspoon salt	
1 tablespoon sugar	3 tablespoons cold water

Sift together dry ingredients. Cut in the suet and add water to form a ball of dough. If parsley is used, add it to the dry ingredients before stirring in the suet and water. This makes one dumpling.

If the pressure cooker method is used, Knaidle may be added to Tzimmes after removing from the cooker. Make several small balls of the dough, tuck them into the carrot and potato combination, then bake 20 to 25 minutes at 375° or till nicely browned on top.

CARROT TZIMMES

5 large carrots (1½ lbs.)
5 medium whole potatoes
3 medium sweet potatoes
2½ to 3 pounds beef brisket (short ribs or "soup meat")
1 teaspoon salt

½ cup sugar or honey
cold water to cover
1 small onion, if desired
2 tablespoons chicken fat or vegetable shortening
2 tablespoons flour

Scrape and slice or dice carrots. Pare and cut potatoes and sweet potatoes into 1-inch rounds. Sear the meat in the pot to be used—a heavy aluminum pot or Dutch oven is best—and when the meat is browned on all sides, add the prepared vegetables, salt and sugar or honey. Cover with cold water about an inch over all and bring to boil over moderate heat. Remove cover and skim. Reduce heat to a simmer and let cook uncovered 2½ to 3 hours or till the meat is very tender. Do not stir the contents of pot. To prevent sticking, shake pot occasionally. Water may be added if necessary a little at a time. If onion is used, it should be peeled and cut into to permit flow of juice and added after boiling begins.

The onion should not be permitted to cook apart but lifted out before it disintegrates. When the liquid has been reduced by half and the meat is tender, brown the flour in melted shortening in a frying pan or shallow saucepan and stir in about a half cup of liquid from pot to make a smooth thickening. Add this thickening to the Tzimmes and shake the pot slightly to distribute evenly. Turn the mixture into a casserole or baking pan and bake 30 minutes at 350° or till brown on top.

Pressure Cooker Method: Sear the meat in the cooker first, then let cool. Add the prepared vegetables, salt, sugar and onion (if used) and 1 to 1½ cups cold water. Cook according to directions for cooker (15 lbs. pressure—20 minutes). Cool under cold water before turning contents into casserole for baking as above. Thickening may be added just before placing in the oven or under broiler flame till lightly browned.

Serves 6.

PRUNE AND POTATO TZIMMES

2 pounds brisket of beef
1 onion, diced
1½ pounds potatoes
1 pound large prunes, rinsed in hot water
cold water to cover
½ teaspoon salt

½ teaspoon cinnamon or dash of nutmeg
½ cup honey, syrup or dark brown sugar
2 tablespoons hot melted shortening (chicken fat preferred)
2 tablespoons flour

Sear the meat on all sides and add the finely diced onions, turning meat till onions and meat are nicely browned. Use the heavy pot in which this Tzimmes is to be cooked. If small potatoes are used, pare, rinse and add whole. If large potatoes are preferred, cut into 1½ inch cubes. Add potatoes to the meat and then the drained prunes. Cover with cold water and cook over moderate heat, uncovered, for 45 minutes. Add the seasonings and sweetening, reduce heat to a mild simmer, adjust the cover on the pot so that steam will escape, to prevent sogginess, and cook 45 minutes to one hour longer.

If additional water is required, small amounts of boiling water may be added as required to prevent scorching. Add the liquid at side of contents in pot and shake the pot gently to distribute. This mixture must not become soupy or mushy. *Do not stir it.* Shake the pot gently during the cooking process. To make the thickening or *einbren,* heat the shortening in a frying pan and stir in the flour till lightly browned. Add about half a cup of liquid from the Tzimmes, stirring in till thick and free from lumps. Add and shake pot gently to distribute this thickening. Let cook three to five minutes before serving. Serve as main dish or poultry accompaniment.

Serves 4 to 6.

PRUNE AND RICE TZIMMES

2 pounds brisket of beef or short rib cross cut	1 cup long-grain rice
	1 teaspoon salt
1 onion	¼ teaspoon cinnamon
½ pound large prunes, rinsed and drained	1 teaspoon grated lemon rind
	2 tablespoons lemon juice
	water

Braise the meat until nicely browned on all sides, and add the ingredients in the order listed. Cover with cold water and cook over moderate heat for 30 minutes in a covered pot. Uncover and add a little boiling water to prevent sticking, shaking the pot gently. Do not stir the mixture. Continue cooking over low heat 1 hour until the meat is tender. The onion may be removed at this point. Turn the mixture into a casserole and bake 25 minutes at 350° or until nicely browned on top and the liquid almost completely absorbed. Or slip the casserole under the broiler flame before serving, to brown on top.

Serves 4 to 6.

RUTABAGA TZIMMES

2 pounds brisket of beef	a dash of nutmeg (optional)
1 onion, diced	½ cup honey, brown sugar, syrup
2 pounds rutabaga, cut into thin	or molasses
inch squares or diced	2 tablespoons hot melted chicken
water to cover	fat
1 teaspoon salt	2 tablespoons flour

Braise the meat and diced onion in the pot to be used. When nicely browned, add the prepared rutabaga and water to cover. Bring to a quick boil, skim well, then turn down heat to keep to a mild boil. Add salt, nutmeg and sweetening and cook 1 hour, shaking the pot occasionally to prevent scorching. Should more liquid be required, add boiling water a little at a time. The vegetable turns a golden orange when done. And this dish is done when the meat is tender enough to pierce with a fork. To further enhance its flavor, make an *einbren* by combining the shortening and flour in a small saucepan or frying pan, stirring till brown. Add this to the Tzimmes, shaking the pot to distribute the thickening evenly. Cook 5 minutes longer on top of stove or turn the mixture into a casserole, meat on top, and brown lightly under the broiler flame just before serving time.

Serves 4 to 6.

FRUITED BUCKWHEAT GROATS RING

1 cup coarse or whole groats	2 eggs
(kasha)	2 tablespoons sugar
1 egg, slightly beaten	¼ teaspoon cinnamon
1 medium-size onion, finely diced	¼ cup each, chopped nuts and
4 tablespoons shortening (oil or	seeded raisins
vegetable)	1 tablespoon candied citron, op-
1 teaspoon salt	tional
4 cups boiling water	2 tablespoons fine crumbs (crack-
	er, bread or matzo meal)

Combine groats with the beaten egg in a large mixing bowl and let stand while frying the diced onion in hot melted shortening or oil. Stir in the egg-coated groats as soon as the onion is lightly browned. Add salt and boiling water, stirring frequently till there are no lumps. Let cook over moderate heat 10 minutes, well covered.

Beat the eggs and sugar in a mixing bowl with a fork or rotary beater and stir into the cooked groats as soon as cool. Stir in the cinnamon, chopped nuts, raisins and citron (finely cut) and pack into a well greased 9-inch ring mold. Sprinkle top with crumbs or matzo meal.

Set the filled ring mold in a pan of water which comes at least one inch up the side of the mold. Bake 30 minutes at 350° or till nicely browned on top. Keep hot till serving time. To unmold, place a large round serving plate over the ring mold and hold together both plate and mold while inverting quickly.

If contents do not turn out easily, wring out a wet towel and place it over the bottom of the upturned mold for a few minutes. The Kugel-in-the-Round should unmold easily. Serve with applesauce, crushed pineapple sauce, raisin sauce or lemon or orange sauce. Also good with canned whole cranberry sauce. Or serve plain with a light dusting of confectioners' sugar.

Serves 6.

NOODLE KUGEL-IN-THE-ROUND

8 ounces broad noodles	½ cup chopped blanched almonds
3 eggs	½ cup seedless raisins
4 tablespoons sugar	½ teaspoon grated lemon rind
¼ teaspoon cinnamon	1 tablespoon lemon juice
4 tablespoons dry crumbs (cracker or bread)	4 tablespoons melted shortening, oil or schmaltz

Cook broken noodles in rapidly boiling salted water as per directions on package, approximately 10 minutes. Drain in a colander and rinse with running hot water for one minute. Drain well. Beat eggs and sugar in a mixing bowl, add cinnamon and half the amount of crumbs. Turn in the drained cooked noodles and stir lightly with two forks. Add almonds and raisins, grated lemon rind and lemon juice while mixing. Heat the shortening in a 9-inch baking ring pan and add to the noodle mixture, stirring in lightly before filling the greased ring. Sprinkle remaining crumbs on top and set the ring in a large baking pan half filled with water. Bake 45 minutes at 400° or till beginning to brown on top. Remove from pan of water and return to stove to brown top of Kugel for about 10 minutes. Serve hot with or without fruit sauce of your choice.

Serves 6 to 8.

PAGEANT SALAD (Basic Recipe)

1 cup grated cooked beets, tightly packed	½ cup canned pineapple syrup
1 cup chopped green pepper	¼ cup mayonnaise or thick salad dressing
1 cup diced tart apple	lettuce cups or shredded salad greens
1 cup drained crushed canned pineapple	slivered almonds or pecan halves for garnish

Combine beets, green pepper, apple and crushed pineapple in a bowl and chill at least one hour before serving time. Combine pineapple syrup

and mayonnaise or thick salad dressing. Place a mound of the salad mixture on lettuce or other greens, either on a large salad plate or individual salad plates. Top with dressing and garnish with almonds or pecan halves.
Serves 6 to 8.

SUNBURST SALAD (Basic Recipe)

2 large grapefruits
2 large seedless oranges
shredded salad greens
½ cup salad dressing

½ cup thick applesauce
chopped nuts
4 canned apricot halves
4 maraschino cherries

Peel grapefruit and remove segments from membrane. Peel and slice oranges as thin as possible. Arrange alternate segments of grapefruit and sliced orange on salad greens for individual salads, or on a large round serving plate in a ring about 3 inches from the rim. Combine salad dressing (or mayonnaise) with applesauce and place a mound of this mixture in the center of salad. Garnish with a sprinkling of chopped nuts and arrange apricot halves around on the large salad plate, or one apricot half in center of each individual salad. Place a maraschino cherry in cavity of apricot, or on top of skin side of fruit.
Serves 4 to 6.
During Passover substitute for the canned fruits.

APPLE FLUDEN (Basic Recipe)

3 cups sifted all-purpose flour
1 teaspoon baking powder
½ teaspoon salt

6 tablespoons melted vegetable
    shortening
¾ cup orange juice

Sift together the dry ingredients. Cut in the melted shortening with a fork or pastry blender till the mixture forms tiny balls. Stir in orange juice gradually to form a ball of dough firm enough to roll out. Divide dough into 3 parts and roll out one to fit into a 9-inch square baking pan, bringing up dough about halfway, pressing it against the sides of pan. Spread with *Filling No. 1*. Roll out the next ball of dough and fit it over the filling. Prick with tines of fork in several places. Spread *Filling No. 2* and cover with the rolled out remaining dough, fluting the edges with fingers, fork or fluting knife. Pierce top layer of dough in flower or leaf design, brush with orange juice or diluted egg yolk and bake 45 to 50 minutes at 350° or till lightly browned on top and the edges begin to stand away from pan.

Filling No. 1

¾ cup seeded raisins, tightly packed
2 cups thin-sliced tart apple, tightly packed
4 tablespoons sugar
½ teaspoon cinnamon
3 tablespoons fine cracker or bread crumbs
1 teaspoon grated lemon peel

Combine and spread evenly over layer of dough.

Filling No. 2

8 ounces red raspberry preserves
¼ cup fine crumbs
½ cup chopped walnuts or almonds

Combine and spread lightly over second layer of dough.
Serves 9.

STANGERL, HUNGARIAN NUT AND CRUMB BARS

4 egg whites
a pinch of salt or cream of tartar
2 cups sugar
½ teaspoon grated lemon rind
1 tablespoon lemon juice
1 pound almonds or walnuts (or 50/50 combination)
1½ cups fine crumbs, toasted

Beat egg whites with salt or cream of tartar till stiff enough to hold a peak. Add the sugar a little at a time till well combined. Add lemon rind and juice. Fold in the nuts which have been put through the fine blade of a grinder and add the toasted crumbs a little at a time till the mixture is thick enough to spread in a thin layer on the bottom of a 9 x 12 inch baking pan, lined with aluminum foil or waxpaper. Top with the following mixture:

Topping

4 egg whites
a pinch of salt
1 cup powdered sugar

Beat egg whites and salt till stiff enough to hold a peak and add the powdered sugar gradually while beating at least 3 minutes by hand with a rotary beater or fork.

Spread the topping evenly over dough in the pan and bake 15 to 18 minutes at 350° or till lightly browned. Cut in the pan while warm, making 1 x 2-inch *stangerl,* or fingers.

Yields 54 pieces.

TAYGLACH (Traditional Method)

3 eggs
2 cups sifted flour sifted with 2
  teaspoons baking powder
1/4 teaspoon salt

1/2 teaspoon ground ginger (or
  nutmeg)
1/2 cup slivered or chopped
  almonds

Beat eggs slightly in a mixing bowl. Sift together dry ingredients, except almonds. Stir into the eggs to form a stiff dough. Turn out on a lightly floured board and knead 1 or 2 minutes. Pat into 1/2-inch thickness a small ball of this dough and roll into pencil-thin lengths. Cut into 1/4-inch or 1/2-inch pieces. Do the same with the rest of the dough. Or roll out the dough into 1/2-inch thickness and cut into 1/4-inch or 1/2-inch squares.

Honey Syrup

1 pound honey
1 cup sugar

1 teaspoon ground ginger

Bring honey, sugar and ginger to a rolling boil in a deep pot and drop the bits of dough in a few at a time to prevent lowering the temperature of the syrup. Cook over reduced heat after all the Tayglach are immersed 20 minutes, using a wooden spoon to push back the mixture, preventing boiling over. Turn out on a wet board and pat into even thickness—about 1/2 inch. Spread the slivered almonds on top, pat smooth with the bowl of a wooden spoon dipped in cold water. Let cool before cutting into small squares or diamond shapes, 1- or 1 1/2-inch size. Or cut into finger lengths 1 inch wide. As soon as cold, Tayglach may be stored in a crock.
Yields 100 to 150, depending on size.

TAYGLACH (Oven Method)

4 eggs
1/4 teaspoon salt

2 1/4 cups flour (approximately)
1 teaspoon baking powder
1 teaspoon vanilla

Beat eggs and salt in a mixing bowl, adding the flour sifted with baking powder and add vanilla a little at a time while mixing, to form a compact ball of dough that can be handled without sticking. Form the dough into balls the size of hazelnuts.

Syrup

1 pound honey	1 teaspoon ginger
1 cup sugar	1/4 cup chopped nuts or shredded coconut

Combine honey, sugar and ginger in a 2-inch deep baking pan. Any size will do if it permits including all the balls of dough without crowding. Heat the oven to 350°. Heat syrup in the pan for 3 minutes before adding the balls of dough. Return to oven and bake 25 minutes or till the syrup has been reduced and the Tayglach are nicely browned. This requires watching, as honey syrup has a tendency to burn. Remove from oven, turn out on a wet or greased kneading board. Separate the Tayglach, dropping each into a bowl of chopped nuts or shredded coconut. Place the coated Tayglach on waxpaper or aluminum foil till dry enough to store in candy boxes or in any other container which can be kept closed till serving time. These keep like candy.

Yields 100 to 150, depending on size.

TAYGLACH MIT NESHOMAS (Tayglach with Souls)

3 cups sifted flour	4 eggs
1 teaspoon baking powder	1/4 teaspoon salt

Sift together flour and baking powder. Beat eggs with salt and combine to make a stiff dough which should be kneaded on a lightly floured board till smooth, free from lumps. Roll out to 1/8-inch thickness and cut into 1 1/2-inch squares, or use a glass to cut rounds.

Filling

1 cup chopped nuts and raisins	1 teaspoon lemon juice

Place a bit of the filling in center of each and fold dough around to make a compact ball or Taygle. Arrange on a greased cookie sheet and bake 20 minutes at 350° or till lightly browned.

Syrup

1 cup honey	1/2 cup water
1 cup sugar	1 teaspoon ground ginger

Combine honey, sugar, water and ground ginger in a large pot and bring to a quick boil, greasing rim of pot to prevent boiling over. Drop in one Taygle at a time, reduce heat to a mild simmer and cook 15 minutes or till the syrup has been absorbed. Shake pot to prevent sticking during the process. Turn out on a large platter dusted with confectioners' sugar and separate these confections before they harden. Should be glossy when cold.

Variation: Substitute 1 whole blanched and peeled almond per Taygle for above filling.

Yom Kippur, Day of Atonement

This is the day of total abstinence from food and drink, the most solemn holy day in the Jewish calendar of holidays. The fast begins at sundown of Yom Kippur Eve and ends with sundown of the next day, after the blowing of the ram's horn at the conclusion of the Yom Kippur Services in Temple or Synagogue.

As common sense dictates, it is well to omit from the Yom Kippur Eve meal all spicy and highly seasoned food. It is wise to undersalt even the Gefilte Fish, and eliminate such thirst-producers as pickles and olives.

In Grandmother's day, it was the custom to stud a quince or orange with cloves and carry it along to Services. The aroma was subtle, reminiscent of the ancient homeland of the Jewish people.

Special care was taken to refill the *P'sommin* Box, or *Uddis*, a silver filigree spice box, so that the house was fragrant with faraway memories of ancient days. On the day of fasting and prayer, of soul-searching and forgiveness, the fragrance of fruit and spices is in keeping with the solemnity of the holiday.

Suggested Menus for Yom Kippur Eve

Menu 1	Menu 2
Grapefruit	Fruit Juice
Gefilte Fish	Chopped Beef Liver Canapés
Chicken Soup with Noodles	Roast Turkey, Cranberry Sauce
Boiled Chicken	Raw Carrot Salad
Peas and Carrots	Hot or Cold Beverage
Mixed Greens Salad	Mandelbrodt
Hot or Cold Beverage	
Cookies or Small Cakes	

Suggested Menus for Yom Kippur Night

For breaking the fast, the menu should include something specially appetizing and zippy as a starter.

Menu 1	Menu 2
Chopped Herring Canapés	Gefilte Fish, Pickled Beet
or Pickled Smelts	Relish or Horseradish
Soup (reheated)	Sliced Turkey or Chicken
Roast Chicken with Dressing	(reheated or cold)
(reheated)	Whole Cranberry Sauce
Cabbage and Cranberry Slaw	Sunburst Salad
Hot or Cold Beverage	Hot or Cold Beverage
Honey Cake	Shtrudel

CHOPPED HERRING (Gehackte Herring)

1 large milch herring, filleted	2 tablespoons oil
2 hard cooked eggs	2 tablespoons sugar
1 tart apple, pared and cored	3 tablespoons dry crumbs or
1 small onion (optional)	matzo meal
2 tablespoons lemon juice or 3	a dash of pepper (optional)
tablespoons mild vinegar	minced parsley or fresh dill

Chop filleted herring that has been soaked overnight. Add hard-cooked eggs, grated tart apple and onion and chop to a smooth pulp. Add remaining ingredients in the order listed, tasting to make sure of exact flavorings. Cover and store in the refrigerator ½ hour before serving. Use as canapé spread or on lettuce as an appetizer.

Serves 2 to 4 as an appetizer, or 6 to 8 as a canapé spread.

Herring in Wine Sauce makes excellent canapés as well as appetizers. Herring should be soaked overnight and washed carefully under running cold water. *Remove head, fins, tail and entrails, before soaking to facilitate handling.* Fillet and cut into strips or serving portions. Place in a wide-mouthed glass jar or other container. Make a marinade of equal parts vinegar and/or lemon juice, brown sugar to taste and any dry wine or sherry. Add the mashed herring milt, one or two bay leaves and a small red pepper to the container of prepared herring and cover with the marinade. Let stand at least 2 hours before serving. A plastic toothpick in each piece facilitates serving.

SUCCOTH, FEAST OF BOOTHS

This holiday is celebrated for a whole week beginning the 15th day of *Tishri,* the seventh month of the Hebrew calendar. It is in commemoration of the first stopping place of the Israelites on their flight from Egypt, according to Biblical accounts.

Today the *Sukkah,* Booth of Willows, is generally constructed close to the Synagogue or Temple for common use, replacing the individual *Sukkah* formerly built by each family. The *Sukkah* is covered with willow branches on top and sides. The branches are placed so that the heavens above may be visible. Inside it is decorated with shucks and ears of corn, pumpkins, squash of all colors, festoons of cranberries, clusters of green, red and dark blue grapes, green- and red-cheeked apples, oranges, grapefruits and any other available fruits and vegetables of the harvest season.

In the *Sukkah,* even when no meals are eaten, a blessing is made over wine in keeping with the holiday. It is the ingathering of the harvest.

Where it is not feasible to erect a *Sukkah,* the dining room of a home or apartment is decorated to simulate a Booth of Willows, and fruit and vegetable decorations are in accordance with the happy occasion.

As a centerpiece for the table, it has become customary to have a "horn of plenty" made of reed or cardboard and aluminum foil. It is filled to overflowing with small fruits and every variety of grapes attainable. Small golden pumpkins, cut into halves and filled with contrasting colored "fruit-of-the-vine," grapes, serve as a basket for harvest decorations.

Religious schools make this holiday the occasion for bringing baskets of fruit to Children's Homes, or to the shut-ins in their communities. In some schools the children bring their offerings of fruits and vegetables to the altar or assembly room dais for the special children's Succoth Service. Such offerings are later distributed to institutions in the community.

MEAT-FILLED KREPLACH

2 cups sifted flour
2 eggs

2 to 3 tablespoons cold water

Filling

1½ cups chopped cooked soup
meat or chicken

1 egg and ¼ teaspoon onion salt

Make a well in the center of the mound of flour in a mixing bowl or on a kneading board. Add the eggs and combine with a fork, adding a little of the cold water at a time while mixing until it forms a compact ball of dough which can be kneaded until smooth and elastic. Roll out on the kneading board, using a rolling pin until the round of dough is as thin as possible. Roll the dough from the outer edge toward center, turning the board as necessary to achieve easier rolling until the sheet of dough is evenly thin. Cut away any lumpy outer edges that remain.

Now cut the dough round or rectangle into 2-inch squares and place a small ball of the meat filling in the center of each. Pinch together two opposite points, then the two sides, to form puffed triangles. Bring two points together to form cap-like Kreplach if desired. Drop the Kreplach one by one into rapidly boiling salted water and reduce heat as soon as the last one is in so that it boils steadily but gently for 15 to 20 minutes. Kreplach rise to the top when done and can be skimmed out or drained. Yields 24 to 36, depending on thickness.

HOLISHKES

(Chopped Meat Wrapped in Cabbage Leaves)

2 pounds chopped beef
¼ cup uncooked brown rice
2 eggs
1 large onion, grated
1 medium carrot, grated
½ teaspoon salt

1 head cabbage (20 to 24 leaves)
½ cup vinegar or ¼ teaspoon
citric acid crystals (sour salt)
¾ cup brown sugar
1 cup canned tomato sauce
cold water to cover

Combine chopped meat, rice, eggs, grated vegetables and salt. Pour boiling hot water over cabbage leaves, cover and let stand until wilted. Drain the water from the cabbage leaves, and when cool enough to handle, place a ball of the meat mixture in the center of a leaf and roll up, tucking in the edges. Place each rolled-up cabbage leaf close to the next one in a large, deep frying pan (the heavier the frying pan the better for the purpose) and add the remaining ingredients listed to cover amply. Cover the pan and cook over moderate heat 30 minutes, then reduce heat for the next 20 minutes. Uncover. Add water if necessary to prevent sticking to the pan, and bake at 350° for 20 minutes or until nicely browned on top. Turn once to brown the under sides if desired. The gravy should be thickened if served separately.

Serves 8 to 10.

SWEET-SOUR POT ROAST   (Basic Recipe)

4½ to 5 pounds beef shoulder	¾ cup dark brown sugar
2 tablespoons oil or schmaltz	½ teaspoon paprika
1 large onion, diced fine	2 tablespoons flour for gravy
1 cup cider vinegar	

Pat the meat dry with paper towel and sear on all sides in heated fat in a heavy kettle that has a close-fitting cover. When nicely browned, add the diced onion and reduce heat till the onions are tender—approximately 3 minutes—stirring two or three times during the process to prevent scorching. Add the vinegar and sugar, sprinkle on the paprika, cover tightly and let simmer 3 hours or till the meat can be pierced with a fork. Mix the flour with a little cold water to form a smooth paste and stir into the gravy after lifting out the meat. Cook for 5 minutes, stirring till smooth. Slice the meat and return to the gravy to keep hot till serving time. Garnish with parsley, plain boiled potatoes or small grated potato pancakes, and serve any favorite salad for a complete meal.

Serves 6 to 8.

LINZER TARTLETS

⅔ cup butter	2 tablespoons grated semi-sweet chocolate
½ cup flour	
⅓ cup sugar	½ cup fine bread or cracker crumbs, sifted
⅔ cup finely ground hazelnuts (almonds may be substituted)	
	¾ cup red raspberry preserves
	1 tablespoon evaporated milk

Use a fork for combining the butter, flour, sugar, ground nuts and chocolate. Add the fine crumbs to make a smooth mixture. Let stand in a cool place 30 minutes before rolling out on a lightly floured board to ⅛-inch thickness. Cut into 1½-inch rounds and place on an ungreased cookie sheet. Bake 12 to 15 minutes at 300°. Let cool before putting two cookies together with some of the preserves to hold them. Brush the tops of the filled cookies with evaporated milk and slip under the broiler flame for a few seconds to glaze. Or return to the top shelf of the oven at 350° for a few seconds.

Yields 18.

LINZER TORTE

1 cup butter or vegetable shortening
1 cup sugar
3 eggs, separated
½ pound blanched almonds, ground
3 tablespoons ground hazelnuts

1 tablespoon grated lemon rind
2 tablespoons juice
2 cups flour, sifted
1 wineglass rum
1 6-ounce glass red raspberry preserves
1 6-ounce glass currant jam

Cream shortening and sugar and add one egg yolk at a time, creaming thoroughly after each addition. Add a little of the ground nuts at a time during the creaming process. Stir in the grated lemon rind and juice, then add the sifted flour gradually, stirring to combine well after each addition. Beat egg whites stiff but not dry, and fold in. Line the bottom of a rectangular baking pan, 9 x 12 or larger, with aluminum foil and press the dough over bottom and an inch up sides. Reserve about ½ cup of the mixture for decorative strips. Sprinkle the rum over the dough before spreading the combined preserves over evenly. Make pencil-thin stripes of reserved dough and place over preserves in lattice formation. Bake 30 minutes at 375° or till light brown on top and at the edges. Cut into 1½-inch squares, when cold, and serve from the pan, using a spatula to lift each piece to a serving plate.

Serves 8 to 12.

HUNGARIAN SOUR CREAM TWISTS

1 cake or package yeast granules
3 tablespoons warm water
1 cup sour cream

4 cups flour, sifted
1 teaspoon salt
½ cup sugar
½ cup butter or substitute

Dissolve yeast in lukewarm water and combine with sour cream. Sift together dry ingredients and cut in the softened shortening till it resembles little peas. Stir in the yeast and sour cream mixture till the batter is smooth. Chill in the refrigerator overnight, or at least 6 hours. Roll out into a rectangle on a kneading board sprinkled with sugar instead of customary flour. Sprinkle more sugar over all, fold right third toward left and fold left third over. Press down with rolling pin and roll over again into a rectangle. Repeat spreading of sugar, folding into thirds and rolling out to make four rollings. Cut into strips 1 inch wide by 3 inches and twist each into any desired form. Place on greased cookie sheet. Let rise 2 hours. Bake at 325° 20 to 25 minutes or till golden brown.

Yields approximately 3 dozen.

CHANNUKAH

This is one of the happiest holidays celebrated by Jews all over the world. It is the Festival of Lights, a commemoration of the restoration of ancient customs which meant continuity of the Jewish people as a people.

The writer Josephus was apparently the first to mention the Feast of Lights, giving credit to Judas Maccabee and the brave fight for religious liberty in the year 165 before the common era. Every year this festival acquires added significance as we re-evaluate our liberties.

A beautiful custom associated with this holiday has been woven into the tradition of the Jewish people: placing the Channukah lights in the nine-branched menorah, where "their lights are for others," near a window. Large electric menorahs are lighted on the grounds of Temples and Synagogues for the week of Channukah.

It has become customary in this country to give Channukah Latke Parties, especially for the children, some time during the holiday week. It presents an opportunity to retell the story of the Maccabees and explain why the lights are kindled, one on the first night, two on the second night, and so forth, till the eighth night.

Channukah food customs include the eating of Latkes, Kugelach, or Kugel. Roast goose, duck, chicken or turkey is used for the feast, either the first night or for the Channukah Sabbath Eve meal.

Roast goose generally serves a double purpose. If the skin and cluster fat are rendered in a special *Pasachdig* (Passover) pot, the strained schmaltz is set aside for Passover use. The cracklings *(greben)* are used in various ways during the week of Channukah.

Wine, cordials, apple cider, fruit juices, tea are the favorite beverages.

Foodlore, handed down from generation to generation, includes an explanation for the eating of Latkes at Channukah time. When the Battle of the Maccabees was at its height, the women behind the lines made the nourishment for their brave fighting men. They mixed batter and baked little flat cakes, Latkes, because that was the quickest way to prepare food. The Grated Potato Latkes are of more recent origin, obviously, as the potato was unknown in Palestine before the discovery of America.

CHANNUKAH DRAIDEL GAME

Draidel games are traditional fun for children and grownups, too.

The Draidel is a four-sided top, made of wood, paper or plastic, with a thumb-piece at the top for spinning it around on the pointed tip. The Draidel falls on one flat side and the marking indicates whether the player has won or lost, and the amount.

Stakes may be peanuts, walnuts, silver or gold-paper-covered chocolate "coins," or pennies. The players start out with an equal number of "coins" and each in turn spins the Draidel. Each adds a number of "coins" to the "kitty" at start of game.

Each of the sides of the Draidel is marked as follows and indicates winnings and losses:

Hebrew *nun* (N) indicates no winnings, no losses.

Hebrew *gimel* (G) indicates player takes all.

Hebrew *hae* (H) directs player to take half the "kitty."

Hebrew *shin* (SH) indicates the player adds one (or any other number previously agreed upon) to the "kitty."

The game may be played until the players decide to quit, and the one who has the largest number of "coins" is declared winner. Or it may be played till one of the players has won all the stakes.

Suggested Menus for Channukah

MENU 1
Broiled Grapefruit Halves
Chopped Beef Liver Canapés
Roast Goose with Dressing
Applesauce
Mixed Greens Salad
Hot or Cold Beverage
Yam Spice Cake

MENU 2
Chicken Soup with Noodles
Roast Chicken with Dressing
Relishes
Brandied Canned Peaches
Hot or Cold Beverage
Fruit Cake

MENU 3
Fruit Juice
Grated Potato Latkes
Applesauce
Cheese and Sour Cream
Hot or Cold Beverage
Fruits in Season

MENU 4
Fruit Juice
Chopped Herring Canapés
Roast Turkey with Dressing
Pickled Pumpkin
Mixed Greens Salad
Hot or Cold Beverage
Cookies

MENU 5
Fruit Cup
Roast Duck Sections with Orange
Pickles, Olives, etc.
Frosted Grapefruit
Hot or Cold Beverages
Scripture Cake

MENU 6
Cabbage Soup
Grated Potato Kugelach
Shaker Cranberry Relish
Hot or Cold Beverage
Fruit Salad and Cookies

GRATED POTATO LATKES (Pancakes)

6 potatoes	½ cup sifted flour
1 onion, grated	½ teaspoon salt
2 eggs	shortening or oil for deep frying

Pare and grate potatoes into a deep bowl. Squeeze some of the liquid out by pressing with the hands or by using a flat grater. Grate in onion, add eggs and flour sifted with salt. Combine thoroughly. Heat shortening in a frying pan and drop the potato batter from a spoon to form flat rounds or ovals. Let fry until crisp at the edges and on under side before turning. Be sure to use sufficient shortening to cover the potato pancakes if you want them to be crisp. Remove pancakes as soon as brown and drain on paper towels. Serve hot with cream cheese, sour cream, applesauce or dried apricot puree.

Serves 6.

GRATED POTATO KUGELACH
(To Serve with Pot Roast Gravy)

Use ingredients, as in recipe above, to form a thick batter. Add 3 tablespoons heated shortening and fill well-greased muffin pans two-thirds full. Bake at 400° 25 to 30 minutes or till nicely browned.

Variation: Instead of vegetable shortening or oil, use chicken or goose schmaltz, including *greben,* well chopped.

APPLE LATKES

1 large tart apple	½ teaspoon salt
¼ cup sugar	1 egg, beaten
1½ cups sifted flour	1 cup milk
1 tablespoon sugar	1 tablespoon melted shortening
1 teaspoon baking powder	a pinch of nutmeg

Core the apple and slice thin without peeling. Sprinkle with sugar and let stand while preparing the batter. Sift together flour, sugar, baking powder and salt into a mixing bowl. Combine beaten egg, milk and melted shortening and stir into the dry mixture to form a thin batter. Season with ground nutmeg. Heat a well-greased griddle or heavy frying pan and pour in a tablespoonful of batter. Place a slice of apple in the center and top with another large tablespoonful of batter. Cook over moderate heat till lightly browned then turn with a pancake turner to brown the other side. Serve hot with a sprinkling of sugar and cinnamon or top with a mixture of sour cream and cottage cheese.

Yields a dozen 4-inch Latkes.

ISRAEL SOOFGANIYAH (Channukah Jelly Doughnuts)

The Sabras, native born Israeli home-makers, have added a special treat to Channukah parties for young and old. Instead of Grated Potato Latkes, they serve these fluffy jelly or jam-filled doughnuts. Here is the recipe and variations you will find helpful:

4½ cups all-purpose flour
1 teaspoon baking powder (phosphate or tartrate type) (¾ teaspoon double-action baking powder)
1¼ cups sugar
1 teaspoon salt
¼ teaspoon nutmeg or cinnamon
2 eggs
¼ cup melted vegetable shortening or oil
1 cup milk, buttermilk or fruit juice
melted shortening or oil for deep frying

Sift flour three times with baking powder, sugar, salt and spice. Combine slightly beaten eggs, cooled melted shortening or oil and the liquid, stirring till the mixture is smooth. Stir into the dry mixture to form a dough that is soft but firm enough to form into balls the size of walnuts or large crabapples. Melt the frying shortening or heat the oil to be used in a deep frying pan to 380° or till hot enough to brown a half-inch cube of dry bread in 25 seconds.

Tuck a bit of strawberry, raspberry or cherry preserves into each flattened ball of dough and cover well by rolling lightly in greased palms. Drop each filled dough-ball into the hot fat and cook over moderate heat 4 to 5 minutes or till nicely browned on all sides. Skim out with a slotted or perforated spoon and drain on paper towels. If a frying basket and deep fryer is used, lift up basket to drain well, then turn out fried doughballs on a large platter dusted with confectioners' sugar. Or dust with the sugar when all the doughballs or *soofganiyah* are cooked and ready to serve.

Makes 36 to 40.

Variation 1: Prune-filled Soofganiyah may be made by tucking into the center of slightly larger balls of dough a soaked, drained and pitted prune. Fry as in basic recipe. Or use pitted dates for filling.

Variation 2: For special parties, place a pecan half or whole blanched almond into center of each pitted prune or date.

Variation 3: Use yeast dough of your choice (see Index). Pinch off balls of dough, insert your favorite filling and form into slightly flattened cakes not more than 1½ inches in size. Prepare all before cooking. Drop into hot frying fat and cook 8 to 10 minutes over moderate heat, or till nicely browned on all sides. These rise to the top of fat as they cook. *Do not overcrowd.* Drain well. Dust with confectioners' sugar while hot and serve. These can be reheated in a moderate oven, but are best eaten when freshly made.

DRAIDLE SANDWICHES

Cut thin slices of white or wholewheat bread. Trim off crust from three sides. Cut fourth side from both ends to form a point, making each slice a five-sided piece, or Draidle shape. Put together with filling and weight under a heavy plate till serving time. If sandwiches are prepared more than an hour before serving, it is best to wrap them in aluminum foil or waxpaper and refrigerate. Use a strip of green pepper for Draidle holder on straight side and garnish with pimiento strips in the form of one or all four of the Draidle letters—N (nun), G (Gimel), H (Hae) and $H (Shin), making four varieties.

Cut sliced bread into 3- or 4-inch rounds and an equal number to be pressed into six-pointed stars with a cookie cutter not larger than the rounds. Put together with any desired filling. Decorate with Hebrew letters of the Draidle, using strips of pimiento, or a thin stream of tomato catsup squeezed through a pastry tube. For sweet-filled sandwiches, press a thin slice of candied cherry or maraschino cherry into center of star.

Make sandwiches of two kinds of bread for variation.

ROAST GOOSE IN A BLANKET

After preparing the goose by removing all feathers, singeing, soaking and salting (in accordance with the rules of Kashrut), cut off the heavy layers of skin and fat. Cut the skin and fat into small pieces before rendering with sliced onion. Reserve the neck skin for stuffing.

Cook the giblets, neck bone and wing tips in enough cold water to cover well, adding a small carrot, onion, celery and parsley. When the gizzard is tender, strain well.

Use the liquid as a basis for gravy and dice the heart and gizzard to be added to the stuffing or to the gravy, as desired.

Use the liver for chopped liver canapés after broiling, chopping and adding mashed hard-cooked egg, minced parsley and some of the rendered schmaltz, with or without a few chopped *greben.*

Rub the inside and outside of goose with a cut clove of garlic or sprinkle with garlic powder mixed with a little flour and paprika.

Make a biscuit dough by mixing 2½ cups flour, 1 teaspoon salt, 1 teaspoon baking powder and 3 tablespoons rendered schmaltz until it forms particles the size of peas. Add approximately ¼ cup ice water and form a ball of dough compact enough to roll out to half-inch thickness. Place this "blanket" over the breast and tuck under the goose before placing in a roasting pan.

Roast the goose-in-a-blanket at 325°, allowing 30 minutes per pound. Be sure to prick the top of "blanket" with a fork in several places to permit steam to escape. You'll like the crispy blanket, too!

If "blanket" is not desired, wrap goose in aluminum foil.

ROAST GOOSE DRESSING
(Basic Bread Crumb Dressing)

1 large onion, diced	½ cup thinly sliced fresh or
4 tablespoons schmaltz	canned mushrooms
1½ cups diced celery, including leaves	2 eggs
	½ teaspoon garlic powder
½ green pepper, diced fine	1 teaspoon salt
½ cup shredded raw carrot	a dash of ginger, white pepper
6 cups dry Challah or other bread crumbs	or paprika

Sauté the diced onion in hot melted schmaltz for two minutes before adding the celery, green pepper and carrot. Stir while cooking over moderate heat for five minutes. Add the bread crumbs and mushrooms and stir for one minute.

Beat eggs in a large mixing bowl and add the ingredients from the frying pan, stirring well. Add the seasonings as soon as the mixture is cool. If the mixture is too dry, a half cup of hot soup, or water flavored with a little orange or lemon juice, may be stirred in. The dressing should not be a compact mass but soft enough to hold its shape when formed into a ball for filling the cavity.

Sew up goose or fasten with polished toothpicks or small skewers before wrapping in aluminum foil or the biscuit dough blanket.

ROAST CHICKEN (Basic Recipe)

6 pound roasting chicken, prepared for the oven

Pat chicken dry with paper towel. Dust inside with a little seasoned flour before stuffing with any of the following dressings. Dust with seasoned flour after sewing up cavity and neck skin. Drizzle a little chicken fat over all and roast in an open roasting pan, allowing 30 to 35 minutes per pound at 325° or till nicely browned. Use double quantity of dressing for goose.

Serves 6 to 8.

Noodle Dressing

2½ to 3 cups broken broad noodles, boiled in salted water and drained
2 eggs
4 tablespoons dry bread or cracker crumbs
1 large onion, diced fine

3 tablespoons schmaltz or other shortening
1 tablespoon grated lemon rind (optional)
¼ teaspoon poultry herb seasoning (optional)
2 tablespoons sugar

Be sure to rinse the cooked noodles in running hot water to remove the starchiness. Add eggs and mix with a fork. Stir in dry crumbs. Brown the diced onion in schmaltz and add while hot, together with the grated lemon rind or herb seasoning, if used. Add sugar last and mix well. Fill cavity of bird and fasten skin with small metal skewers or polished wooden toothpicks. Or sew up with needle and strong white thread.

Potato-Prune Dressing

1½ cups mashed white potatoes
1½ cups mashed sweet potatoes
2 eggs
12 to 14 large prunes, soaked and pitted

2 tablespoons lemon or orange juice
a dash of cinnamon or nutmeg
¼ cup dry bread or cracker crumbs

Combine ingredients in the order listed.

Whole Wheat Croutons Dressing

3½ to 4 cups diced whole wheat bread
1 large onion, diced fine
4 tablespoons chicken schmaltz

1 cup finely diced celery and/or green pepper
1 carrot, shredded
2 eggs
salt and pepper to taste

Brown the diced bread in the oven, turning once or twice till lightly browned croutons are crisp but not burned. Lightly brown the diced onion in hot fat. Add croutons, stirring lightly for one minute. Add diced celery and/or green pepper and carrot and stir over moderate heat till heated through. Let cool before adding slightly beaten eggs, stirring only till mixed. Taste and season if necessary.

This dressing may be baked, uncovered, in a casserole till lightly browned on top, and served separately. Place it in the oven for 30 minutes at 350° or for 45 minutes at 325° while the poultry is in the oven.

CABBAGE SOUP (Basic Recipe)

1½ pounds cabbage, shredded or chopped	1 diced onion
1 tablespoon salt	1 large carrot, shredded
3 pounds brisket of beef or short ribs	2 quarts hot water
	½ cup vinegar, lemon juice or citric acid crystals as required
	4 tablespoons brown sugar

Sprinkle shredded cabbage with salt and let stand while braising the meat in the heavy pot to be used. Add diced onion and stir till light brown. Add cabbage which has been squeezed to almost dry. Stir well till light brown. Add carrot, hot water, vinegar or lemon juice and brown sugar to taste. If citric acid crystals is the favorite for this dish, be sure to use a little at a time till it is of the desired sourness. Cover and bring to a boil. Reduce heat and let cook slowly 1½ hours or till meat is tender.

Make a thickening *einbren* by browning 2 tablespoons flour in 2 tablespoons schmaltz or salad oil, stirring till light brown. Add 1 cup of the soup, stirring till thick. Turn into the soup after lifting out meat. Slice meat and keep warm in a little of the soup till serving time. Serve hot with plain boiled potatoes.

Serves 6 to 8.

TROPICAL CHANNUKAH SALAD

1-inch thick slices of papaya	shredded salad greens
8 4- or 5-inch sticks of candied fruit peel	4 maraschino cherries
	Pineapple Salad Dressing

Cut papaya melon into rings one inch thick. Remove seeds and cut away outer peeling. Stick the candied fruit peel, which should be dry and colored with vegetable coloring to suit the color scheme, either red, green or orange, into the melon ring. Surround with some shredded salad greens and top each "candle" with half a maraschino cherry half to simulate lights. Make the pineapple salad dressing as follows:

Pineapple Salad Dressing

3 ounces cream cheese	2 tablespoons honey
½ cup canned pineapple juice	lemon or orange juice to taste

Mash cheese with a fork and work in the fruit juice till smooth. Sweeten with honey and add a few drops of lemon or orange juice for added flavor.

CHANNUKAH CANDLE SALADS

Asparagus tips, fresh cooked or canned, may be used to simulate candles. Arrange on shredded lettuce or other salad greens. Tip with a bit of cooked carrot to represent candle flame and garnish with green and red pepper strips at base of candle. Serve with French dressing or mayonnaise.

Banana-pineapple candles can be made easily by standing a 2½-inch cut of peeled banana upright on a slice of canned pineapple. Half a green or red pepper may be cut into strips and adjusted to simulate holders. Tip the banana candles with half a maraschino cherry to resemble flame. Dot the pineapple with mayonnaise to which minced parsley or green and red pepper bits have been added and arrange bits of salad greens around the pineapple on each plate.

Banana menorahs, holding the number of "lights" required, are made by placing peeled bananas, boat fashion, on a bed of salad greens and inserting thin mint candy sticks topped with bits of maraschino cherries. Slicing curved side of banana will prevent tipping. Or place banana curved side up, slicing both ends to prevent slipping. Insert candy candles, etc. Garnish as desired with frozen or canned cherries or berries.

Use a thick slice of canned pineapple as a base for holding mint stick candles, either all eight candles or the number for that night. Place on shredded salad greens and garnish with maraschino cherries or frozen whole strawberries or raspberries, or melon balls. Use any fruit salad dressing with these individual salads.

If cantaloupe or honey dew melons are available in your locality, cut 1-inch thick slices, remove seeds and trim away outer skin. Use as candle base, arranging mint stick candles in a ring. Fill center of ring with berries, cherries or small melon balls.

Use a large cookie cutter for cutting out rounds of sponge cake to use as candle base for mint stick candy candles. Add or pass separately stewed fresh or dried fruits, tinted to fit into the color scheme of the occasion.

YAM SPICE CAKE WITH ORANGE JUICE

1 cup mashed, cooked yams (or red sweet potatoes)
1 cup all-purpose flour
½ teaspoon salt
2 teaspoons baking powder
¼ teaspoon baking soda
¼ teaspoon each allspice and ground cloves
½ teaspoon each, cinnamon and nutmeg
⅓ cup vegetable shortening
1 cup sugar
2 eggs
½ cup each, chopped nuts and seeded raisins (or seedless kind)
⅓ cup of any fruit juice or apple cider

While the mashed sweet potato is getting cool, sift together the dry ingredients into a mixing bowl. In another bowl cream the shortening and sugar till fluffy, then add one egg at a time, beating or mixing till well combined. Stir in the mashed sweet potato and then the sifted dry ingredients, a little at a time, alternately with the liquid used. Reserve a little of the flour mixture to add to the chopped nuts and raisins—a good way to do this is to put the nuts and raisins and a little of the flour mixture into a paper bag and shake to distribute flour evenly. This prevents the nuts and raisins from lumping. Turn this batter into a well-greased and floured 8- or 9-inch square cake pan and bake 35 minutes at 350° or until nicely browned on top. When cool, cut the cake into 2-inch squares in the pan. Lift out each serving and top with the following sauce:

Orange Sauce

1½ cups fresh or canned orange juice	1½ tablespoons cornstarch
1 tablespoon grated orange rind	⅓ cup sugar
	⅛ teaspoon salt
	1 tablespoon lemon juice

Combine all listed ingredients and cook in the top of a double boiler until clear, stirring constantly till thickened. Or stir a little of the fruit juice with the cornstarch to prevent lumps forming when cooking, adding remaining ingredients gradually, then cook over low heat. This must be stirred constantly to prevent scorching.

Yields 1½ cups sauce.

Variation: Add 6 large maraschino cherries cut into thin rounds just before serving this sauce.

APPLESAUCE COOKIES (Basic Recipe)

2 cups all-purpose flour	1 egg
½ teaspoon salt	1 cup sugar
½ teaspoon baking powder	½ cup vegetable shortening or salad oil
1 teaspoon cinnamon	
¼ teaspoon each nutmeg and all-spice	1 cup thick applesauce, canned or fresh
⅔ cup seedless raisins	½ teaspoon baking soda

Sift together dry ingredients and add the raisins, stirring to coat well. Combine egg, sugar and shortening by beating thoroughly. Stir in the applesauce to which baking soda has been added. Add to dry mixture, stirring till well combined. Drop from the tip of a teaspoon on a greased cookie sheet, at least an inch and a half apart each way. Bake 15 minutes at 350° or till lightly browned. When cold, cookies may be tipped with a bit of white frosting and decorated with a sliver of almond or bit of pecan or walnut.

Store these cookies in a well-covered container.

Yields 48 to 60, depending on size.

CHANNUKAH CUPCAKES

½ cup butter or vegetable shortening	¼ cup cream or evaporated milk plus ¼ cup water
1 cup sugar	1½ teaspoons vanilla or almond flavoring
3 eggs	
2 cups all-purpose flour	a pinch of salt if unsalted butter is used
3 teaspoons baking powder	

Cream shortening and sugar. Add one egg at a time, beating well after each addition. Sift together dry ingredients and stir into the creamed mixture alternately with the liquid used. Grease small muffin pans and fill two-thirds full. Bake 15 to 20 minutes at 325° or till lightly browned. Or place fluted paper cups inside muffin pans, for variety, and fill to three-quarters full to bring cupcakes into a peak when baked. Cool before frosting and decorating.

Frosting

1½ cups confectioners' sugar	1 tablespoon lemon juice or 1 teaspoon each vanilla and almond flavoring
3 tablespoons melted shortening	
	a pinch of salt

Combine sugar and shortening till smooth and add, a little at a time, the flavoring used, mixing till of spreadable consistency. Reserve 3 tablespoons of frosting which may be colored with red or blue vegetable coloring and used to form *Mogen Dovids* on each cupcake after the white frosting is set.

Yields 18 to 24.

SESAME COOKIES

2 egg whites	1 cup sifted confectioners' sugar
¼ cup cake flour	¼ teaspoon salt
	1 cup sesame seed

Beat egg whites stiff and dry. Combine flour, sugar and salt and sift together into the beaten egg whites. Fold in lightly with a fork, then add sesame seeds gradually, folding in as lightly as possible. Drop from the tip of a teaspoon on a greased cookie sheet, 2 inches apart each way. Bake 10 minutes at 400°.

Yields approximately 30.

FRIED CRULLER BOWS

2 cups sifted all-purpose flour	1 tablespoon rum or sherry
a pinch of salt	vegetable shortening or oil for
2 eggs	deep frying
3 tablespoons sugar (confectioners' if desired)	confectioners' sugar for dusting bows

Sift together flour and salt into a mixing bowl and make a well in the center. Drop the eggs and sugar into the well and begin stirring till most of the dry ingredients have been absorbed, then add the rum or sherry. Remove the ball of dough to a floured kneading board and knead 3 to 5 minutes. Let stand on board, covered with a towel, at least an hour at room temperature. Divide the dough for convenient rolling into 1/4-inch or thinner rectangles, as large as desired. Dough not rolled should be kept covered with towel till used.

Fold the layer of rolled-out dough into thirds and roll again into any length and thickness desired—about 1/8 inch thick and 4 inches wide is best. Cut into 5-inch strips not more than a half-inch wide, twist each into looped bows as you drop them into deep hot melted fat for cooking over moderate heat till lightly browned. These rise to the top when done and should be skimmed out with a slotted or perforated spoon. Be careful not to overcrowd during the cooking process. Skim out and drain well on paper towels. Dust with confectioners' sugar and serve.

Serves 8 to 12.

FRUIT CAKE

1 pound seedless raisins	1 teaspoon baking soda
1 pound currants	1 teaspoon salt
1 pound prunes, soaked and pitted	1 teaspoon cinnamon
1 pound black mission figs	1 teaspoon allspice
1 cup candied citron, diced fine	1/2 teaspoon nutmeg
1 cup candied orange or grapefruit peel, diced fine	1/2 teaspoon cloves (optional)
2 cups coarsely chopped nuts (walnuts, almonds, etc.)	2 cups vegetable shortening
	2 cups dark brown sugar
6 cups sifted flour	6 eggs
3 teaspoons baking powder	1 cup dark molasses
	1 cup strong coffee
	1/4 cup brandy
	3 tablespoons vanilla extract

Prepare 4 one-pound coffee cans with tight-fitting covers by lining with aluminum foil or greased heavy paper cut to fit. Or use 9-inch loaf pans if more convenient.

Use a kitchen scissors for cutting raisins, prunes and figs into fine bits. Combine with currants and diced candied fruit peels and dust lightly with flour or shake in a paper bag for equal coating. Add chopped nuts of your choice. Sift together all the dry ingredients into a large mixing bowl. Cream shortening and brown sugar and add eggs one at a time, beating well after each addition. Blend in molasses and stir in the sifted dry ingredients a little at a time, alternately with the prepared fruit and nuts combination, stirring well after each addition. Add gradually coffee mixed with brandy and vanilla flavoring as you blend all together into a heavy but evenly mixed batter. Turn into prepared baking tins or loaf pans, filling two-thirds full. Cover tightly, tying heavy aluminum foil over the loaf pans if used.

Place on flat clothespins in shallow pans holding about 2 inches of water. Bake 2 to 2½ hours at 300°, replenishing water if necessary. Remove from water pans and continue baking 45 to 60 minutes longer at 275°. Test before removing from oven by inserting a wooden toothpick in center of cake. If cakes are done, the toothpick will be dry when removed.

Remove covers from baked cakes and let cool in the pans by placing them on wire racks to permit air to circulate under and around. Unmold and remove aluminum foil or greased paper.

If a glaze is desired, prepare the following to pour over cakes:

½ cup honey or dark syrup	3 tablespoons brandy
¼ cup water	

Combine and brush over cakes which have been cooled then returned to the oven on a cookie sheet. Bake 10 to 15 minutes longer at 275°. The glaze may be brushed on several times during this additional baking. When cold, be sure to wrap cakes separately in aluminum foil before returning to tins or pans that have been carefully washed and dried. Wrap containers with cakes with aluminum foil for storing and ripening about two weeks before cutting and serving.

Yields 4 one-pound tins of fruit cake, weighing much more; or 4 loaf fruit cakes.

BLONDE FRUIT CAKE

½ cup butter or substitute (vegetable shortening)	¼ cup each finely cut citron and candied orange peel
1 cup sugar	2 cups sifted flour
½ cup sour cream	¼ teaspoon each salt and baking soda
1 cup each chopped almonds and Sultana raisins	2 teaspoons baking powder
¼ cup finely cut candied cherries (or maraschinos)	5 egg whites
	1 teaspoon vanilla
	1 wineglass good brandy

Cream shortening and sugar, then blend in the sour cream. Combine nuts, raisins and candied fruits with half the sifted flour. Sift together remaining flour with the other dry ingredients. Combine all the mixtures in a large mixing bowl. Beat egg whites stiff and fold in together with the flavoring and brandy, stirring to blend well. Do not beat. Turn the mixture into a well-greased tube cake pan that has been lined with heavy waxpaper or aluminum foil. Bake 2 to 2½ hours at 300°.

Holiday time for the Jewish home-maker means extra baking, of course.

But who wouldn't be proud to have on hand one of those delightful specialties we get from Hungarian kitchens? It is a multi-layered cake called Dobos Torte, the favorite pastry of Hungarian and Austrian Jewish families. Try making this one:

DOBOS TORTE (Multiple-layer Cake)

¾ cup flour, sifted 3 times	1 tablespoon lemon juice
10 egg yolks	6 egg whites
1 pound powdered sugar	¼ teaspoon cream of tartar

Sift flour into a deep mixing bowl. Into another bowl, beat the egg yolks till creamy and lemon-colored, adding sugar a little at a time while mixing (by hand, 15 minutes, in electric mixer, 5 minutes). Sift the flour into the beaten egg mixture gradually, keeping the electric mixer (the rotary beater, if by hand) going about 5 minutes or till well blended. Add the lemon juice, mix a few turns to blend. Beat egg whites and cream of tartar till stiff, and fold into the first mixture with an over and over motion of the mixing spoon or fork. Turn the batter into well-greased and waxpaper-lined 8-inch cake pans, filling 3 pans at a time. Be sure to spread the batter thin, just enough to cover the bottoms of pans evenly. Bake each set of 3 layers 5 minutes, at 450° or till lightly browned at the edges. Remove each set of layers carefully, turning them out on a double fold of cloth or paper towels.

This amount of batter should yield 12 thin layers. Dusting the towels lightly with confectioners' sugar helps a great deal. When all layers are cool, put together with a thin filling of chocolate frosting.

Favorite Chocolate-Rum Filling

½ pound unsalted butter	2 egg yolks
2 cups confectioner's sugar, sifted	3 tablespoons good rum
3 squares of unsweetened chocolate	

Cream the butter, adding sugar gradually till smooth. Do this while melting the chocolate in a saucepan over boiling water. Beat egg yolks till creamy and combine by adding the creamed mixture to the melted chocolate, then stirring in beaten egg yolks and rum till blended. Beat thoroughly till of desired consistency for spreading baked layers. Thin spreading is best for multi-layer cake. Beat remainder till thicker, for topping, in any desired pattern. Or spread top of cake with the thin filling.

Caramel Glaze for Dobos Torte

⅔ cup powdered sugar

1 tablespoon butter or vegetable shortening

Combine in a saucepan and melt over direct low flame, stirring constantly till the mixture takes on a caramel color and is of a pourable consistency. Turn this over the top of Dobos Torte and let run down sides at will. With a knife dipped in hot water, score the glazed top cross-stitch fashion. When serving, dip the cutting knife in boiling water to prevent ragged edges of cut sections of cake.

PICKLED PUMPKIN

3 pounds pumpkin
1½ cups dark brown sugar

¾ cup pickling vinegar
¼ teaspoon allspice
1 teaspoon salt

Cut away skin from pumpkin which can be bought whole or cut by the pound. Dice or cut into small wedges. Make a syrup of vinegar and brown sugar, add allspice and salt and add the prepared pumpkin. Bring to a boil quickly, then reduce heat and cook only till pumpkin pieces are tender enough to pierce with a toothpick. Turn into glass jars and seal.

Yields approximately 1 quart.

FROSTED GRAPEFRUIT

1½ cups apple cider
5 drops red vegetable coloring
6 cups drained canned grapefruit sections

10 or 12 maraschino cherries for topping

Tint the cider and turn into freezing tray of electric refrigerator. Freeze till a mushy consistency, approximately 1½ hours. Spoon grapefruit sections into 10 or 12 sherbet cups just before serving time and add some of the frosted cider. Top each with a maraschino.

Serves 10 to 12.

BRANDIED CANNED PEACHES

1 large can peach halves (8 or 9 peach halves) 8 or 9 cloves	syrup from canned peaches 2- inch stick cinnamon 2 tablespoons lemon juice ¼ cup good brandy

Drain syrup from peaches. Stick a clove in each peach half. Combine syrup, stick cinnamon, lemon juice, and bring to a boil over moderate heat. Pour over prepared peach halves in a glass container and add the brandy. Cover and let stand overnight before serving.

Serves 8 or 9.

SHAKER CRANBERRY RELISH

3 large seedless oranges, unpeeled 3 cups uncooked cranberries 4 tart apples, cored, unpared	1 cup canned shredded pineapple 2¼ cups brown sugar, tightly packed

Put quartered oranges and cranberries through the coarse blade of food chopper. Shred the apples. Combine with canned pineapple and sugar, mixing well. Let stand at room temperature overnight or at least 6 hours before using. Use as a relish with meat or poultry or serve with pancakes.

Serves 8 to 12.

CABBAGE AND CRANBERRY SLAW

3 cups finely shredded cabbage 1 teaspoon salt 1 cup uncooked cranberries, washed, drained and chopped	½ cup commercial salad dressing ¼ cup sour cream 2 tablespoons sugar

Combine all ingredients listed and let stand in the refrigerator about 1 hour before serving on crisp lettuce or other greens as individual salads or in a salad bowl. Goes well with fish meals.

Serves 6 to 8.

Tu b'Sh'vat or Chamiso Oser b'Sh'vat

This is truly an agricultural folk festival, the New Year of the Trees, corresponding to Arbor Day in the United States. It is called *Tu b'Sh'vat* in Israel and is celebrated by the planting of trees where most needed for reforestation and beautification of towns, villages, and public parks and play spaces in the large cities.

The children parade, decked in wreaths of flowers, bearing seedlings or potted plants. Schools are assigned specific localities for the planting of their offerings of growing things, and the parades are watched by adoring and admiring parents and teachers as well as public officials.

In many countries it has become customary to hold public functions on or near the 15th of Sh'vat, some time in January. Money for the planting of trees in Israel is the admission price, or donations of trees in honor or memory of various anniversaries, recovery from illness or as tributes to departed relatives or friends are made through The Jewish National Fund.

A living tree is a living tribute, especially in celebration of *Tu b'Sh'vat* in the new State of Israel.

Food customs include the traditional "rozhinkes mit mandlen" (raisins and almonds of folklore and folksong), and *bokser* (St. John's Bread), along with holiday specials such as Shtrudel.

Purim, Festival of Mirth and Memories

This festival originated about 2,400 years ago, according to scholars and historians. It has ever since been celebrated on the 14th day of the Hebrew month of *Adar,* in every country where Jews live. The drama with a happy ending which took place in the city of Shushan in a country called Persia (now Iran) under the reign of King Ahasuerus, is read aloud from the *Megillah* each year to Jewish congregations.

There have been many Purims in the long record of Jewish history. The Jewish Encyclopedia lists them all from the first to the most recent one, known as *Burgel Purim,* which occurred in Tripoli in 1793. That story tells of a Pasha who, in his declining years, whiled away his time listening to clever stories. During his reign, restrictive measures against Jews became so unbearable that the leaders of the Jewish community felt a catastrophe would befall them if something were not done immediately.

The wife of the leader of the community managed to gain an audience with the Pasha. She had the grace and beauty of Queen Esther of Ahasuerus' reign, and the cleverness of Scheherazade. She became an influence in the life of the Pasha and his court, and like Queen Esther of old, managed to save the Jews of her day from drastic measures against them. This estimable lady lived till 1800.

In 1786 the Jews of Adrianapole in European Turkey miraculously escaped extermination when they were accused of shielding some mountain brigands who had fallen upon the town. When the Jews were exonerated of the crime of subversion, the Council of Rabbis declared a special Purim, known to this day as the Purim of the Bandits.

The Brandeis Purim or *Povidle Purim,* is perhaps best remembered in this country because it originated in the section of Bohemia, in 1731, from which the ancestors of the late Justice Louis Dembitz Brandeis of the U. S. Supreme Court migrated to the western world. There a grocer named Brandeis was accused of the death of a Christian child. When he was found innocent, the day before Purim of the Scroll of Esther, the women of the town filled the Hamantaschen with prune jam, for there was no poppyseed at the grocer's. It has become known as *Povidle Purim* as well as Brandeis Purim among all who hail from that part of the world.

Purim has grown in significance as well as pattern of celebration. In many countries it is carnival time for young and old, with plays and pageants, Queen Esther Balls, exchange of gifts (called *Shalach Monos),* and gifts to the underprivileged. In Israel it has become *Ad-lo-Yadoh,* flinging all care to the winds in the general exuberance of the festival.

Folklore has it that on Purim one must drink to the point where "he know not which is Haman and which is Mordecai." Quips like *"a gantz yohr shikker* and on *Purim nichter"* (drunk the year round but sober on Purim) are still current.

Like all holidays and festivals in the Hebrew calendar, Purim has its special foods. The Hamantaschen may be filled with poppyseeds, honey and fruit, *povidle* or nuts and raisins. They may be three-cornered or shaped like a donkey's ears, elongated, as Italian Jews prefer to make them. Or the treat of the day for children may be little Hamans—gingerbread men—as is the custom in Holland and the Netherlands. *Nahit,* chick peas, also called *garbanzos* in Spanish-speaking countries, and *checci* by Italians, are part of Purim fare. Nuts and raisins, wines, cordials, schnapps, are accompaniments of the other toothsome goodies "full of sugar and spice, and everything nice." For

"Today is Purim—tomorrow it's o'er . . .
Fling us a coin, then show us the door!"

HAMANTASCHEN (Special Yeast Dough)

1 cup milk	¼ cup lukewarm water
¼ cup sugar	1 egg
¼ cup butter or substitute	1 teaspoon vanilla
1 teaspoon salt	2½ cups all-purpose flour
1 cake or package granulated yeast	¾ cup butter or substitute

Combine milk, sugar, butter and salt and heat to lukewarm. Dissolve yeast in lukewarm water and stir into the first mixture. Stir in egg and vanilla flavoring. Sift flour once, then gradually sift into the liquid mixture, beating well after each addition till a ball of dough is formed. Dust with flour, cover with a doubled towel or aluminum foil and let stand at room temperature approximately 2 hours till about double in bulk. Punch dough down before rolling out on a lightly floured cloth or board to ¼-inch thickness, into a rectangular shape for easier handling.

Put bits of butter or substitute lengthwise along the center and fold one-third of the pastry over. Pat down and put more bits of butter along the folded-over strip lengthwise. Fold the upper length of dough over and pat down. Roll from the narrow end toward center with a rolling pin to an even thickness. Dot one half of the pastry with butter, fold over and roll again into a rectangle to the thickness desired for the filling to be used.

For Poppyseed and Honey Filling, the dough should be about ¼-inch thick. For Prune Butter or Prune Jam Filling, make the dough slightly thicker. (See pages 72-73 for fillings.)

Use a biscuit cutter, cookie cutter or thin glass for cutting dough into 2-inch rounds. Roll or flatten each. Place the desired filling in centers and pinch together dough to form triangles, seams from center top to pointed corners. Place these on a lightly greased cookie sheet and let rise away from draughts for about 30 to 45 minutes. Brush tops lightly with evaporated milk or diluted egg yolk and bake 25 to 30 minutes at 375° or till lightly browned.

Yields 24 to 36.

HAMANTASCHEN (Sweet Yeast Dough)

1 cake or package granulated yeast	½ cup salad oil
¼ cup lukewarm water	1 cup lukewarm milk
2 eggs	¾ cup water from boiled potatoes
⅔ cup sugar	1 tablespoon vanilla
2 teaspoons salt	6 cups sifted all-purpose flour

Dissolve the yeast in lukewarm water. Beat eggs with sugar and salt and stir in. Combine oil, lukewarm milk and potato water. Stir into the

first mixture, sifting in the flour gradually till a ball of dough is form
The vanilla flavoring may be added to either of the liquid combinations
or while adding flour. Knead thoroughly on a lightly floured cloth or
board till smooth and elastic. Return to mixing bowl, dust with flour,
cover with a towel or aluminum foil and refrigerate overnight or at least
6 hours.

When ready for baking Hamantaschen, pinch off little balls of
dough, pat or roll out to half-inch thickness or thinner, place filling (see
pages 72-73 for fillings) in center and bring up edges to form three-cornered
filled cakes, pinching together from center top down three sides. Place
on a lightly greased cookie sheet to rise at room temperature till about
double in bulk. Brush with evaporated milk or diluted egg yolk, or fruit
juice of any kind. Bake 30 to 35 minutes at 350° or till lightly browned.

Yields approximately 4 dozen.

HAMANTASCHEN (Cream Cheese Dough)

1 cup softened butter or substi- tute	1/8 teaspoon salt
6 ounces cream cheese	2 1/2 to 3 cups sifted all-purpose flour

This is a very short dough and must be refrigerated before rolling out.
It must be used rapidly, so use a small amount at a time for filling and
shaping. These Hamantaschen should be baked as soon as formed and
as directed below.

Combine butter, cheese and salt in a mixing bowl, then sift in flour,
mixing with a fork or wire pastry blender. Form into a compact but
light ball of dough and chill in refrigerator overnight or at least 2 hours
before using.

Pinch off little balls of dough about the size of a walnut, flatten with
the fingers on a lightly floured board and place a teaspoonful of filling
in centers. Bring up edge to form the three-cornered Hamantaschen and
place on ungreased but lightly floured cookie sheet. Work fast to prevent
dough from becoming too soft. Four hands for this task makes it easier.
Brush the tops of filled Hamantaschen lightly with cream or evaporated
milk for a glaze and bake 12 to 15 minutes at 350° or till lightly browned.
If cookie sheets are covered with aluminum foil, dusting with flour is
not necessary.

For fillings, see pages 72-73.

Yields 24 to 36.

HAMANTASCHEN (Pie Pastry)

...ted flour	2 tablespoons sugar
...on salt	½ cup ice water
¾ c.. ...egetable shortening or salad oil	

Sift together flour and salt in a mixing bowl. Cut in the shortening with two knives or a wire pastry blender till little crumbs the size of small peas are formed. Stir in the sugar and cold water a little at a time, mixing lightly till combined, firm enough to roll out on a lightly floured board to ⅛-inch thickness. Or chill the dough about 1 hour for best results. Cut the ball of dough into 3 or 4 parts for easier handling when making Hamantaschen. Cut into 2½-inch rounds, or smaller, with a thin wine glass. Top each with a little filling (see below). Bring up the edges to form three-cornered filled pastries. Press together, making the seams from center down three sides. Place on a cookie sheet, brush tops with diluted egg yolk and bake at 425° 12 minutes or till nicely browned.

These Hamantaschen should be served warm. They can be reheated, however, by placing in a 350° oven for a few minutes just before serving time.

Yield depends on thickness of pastry dough and type of filling used.

FILLINGS FOR HAMANTASCHEN

Poppy Seed and Honey

2 cups poppy seed	¼ cup sugar
1 cup milk or water	⅛ teaspoon salt
½ cup honey	2 eggs (optional)

If poppy seeds are the large variety, scald, drain well, then pound to a pulp or put through fine blade of a food chopper. Combine with liquid, honey, sugar and salt and cook over low heat till thick. This requires careful watching to prevent scorching. Stir frequently while cooking. Let cool before beating in eggs if used. Fine poppy seeds can be used without pounding or grinding.

Prune Butter (Lacqua or Povidle)

1½ to 2 cups thick prune butter	½ cup ground blanched almonds
4 tablespoons fine cake or dry bread crumbs	¼ teaspoon salt
	1 tablespoon grated lemon or orange rind

Combine thoroughly by mixing with a fork.
Variation 1: Add ½ cup finely chopped walnuts to either filling.
Variation 2: Add ½ cup finely chopped seedless raisins to either filling.

Homemade Povidle (Prune Jam)

2 pounds large-size prunes	½ cup honey
hot water to cover	¼ teaspoon cinnamon

Rinse the dried prunes under running hot water and drain. Place prunes in a glass container, cover with boiling water, let stand till cool, then place in the refrigerator overnight. In the morning they should be soft enough to remove pits easily. Put through a fruit press or use a food chopper for making it into pulp. Add honey and cinnamon and cook over low heat, stirring constantly till thickened and firm enough to hold its shape when dropped from the tip of a teaspoon. Or spread to an even thickness in a baking pan and bake 30 to 45 minutes at 350° or till the mixture is thickened to the desirable consistency. This must also be watched carefully to prevent scorching.

Mixed Dried Fruits

1 pound pitted prunes	2 tablespoons lemon juice
½ pound dried apricots	¼ cup brown sugar
¼ pound dried pears	a dash of nutmeg
1 seedless orange, quartered, unpeeled	4 tablespoons dried cracker crumbs
grated rind of 1 lemon	

Put the dried fruits and orange through the medium blade of a food chopper and add remaining ingredients in the order listed. Taste and add sugar if necessary.

The above amounts of filling will be sufficient for 24 to 36 small Hamantaschen or 20 to 30 larger ones.

PURIM STOLLEN (Quick and Easy)

1 egg	3 tablespoons melted butter or substitute
⅓ cup evaporated milk	2 cups prepared biscuit mix
¼ cup sugar	

Beat egg slightly in a bowl and stir in evaporated milk, sugar, melted butter or substitute and stir in biscuit mix to make a stiff dough. Turn out on a lightly floured board and knead gently. Roll out to a rectangle, 9 x 15 inches, and brush lightly with either evaporated milk or melted shortening.

Filling

grated rind of 1 lemon	⅓ cup apricot or prune jam
2 tablespoons lemon juice	3 tablespoons fine crumbs
3 tablespoons sugar	3 tablespoons chopped walnuts
	½ cup poppy seeds (fine variety)

Combine lemon rind and juice of lemon. Add sugar, apricot or prune jam (*povidle*), crumbs, nuts and poppy seeds.

Spread half the filling mixture along the long side of rectangle of dough, starting an inch from the edge, to about the middle. From the opposite side, spread the filling toward the center within 2 inches of filling already spread. Roll up both sides toward center, then fold over. Place on a greased baking pan, brush with evaporated milk or butter and sprinkle with poppy seeds, if desired. Bake 15 to 18 minutes at 425° or till nicely browned. Cut diagonally into 1½-inch slices. Serve warm. Serves 10.

PURIM SWIRL COOKIES (Raised Dough)

½ package granulated yeast	⅓ cup sugar
⅔ cup lukewarm milk or fruit juice	1 cup vegetable shortening
1 teaspoon sugar	2 eggs, slightly beaten and stirred
2½ cups sifted all-purpose flour	into liquid mixture
½ teaspoon salt	½ teaspon vanilla or grated rind
	of 1 lemon

Dissolve yeast in lukewarm liquid, adding teaspoon sugar. Sift together flour, salt and sugar and cut in the shortening with a wire pastry blender or use fingers. Add eggs, dissolved yeast and liquids, stirring till the mixture forms a soft dough. Knead, working in grated lemon rind or vanilla, smooth and elastic. Place in a well-greased bowl, cover with a doubled towel and let rise about 1 hour at room temperature, away from drafts.

Roll out about a third of the dough at a time into rectangles ¼-inch thick and spread with the following filling:

1½ cups poppyseeds, ground or mashed	1 tablespoon lemon juice
1 cup sugar	1 teaspoon grated lemon rind. (optional)
	½ cup fruit juice or milk

Combine ingredients in top of double boiler and cook over boiling water till thick enough to spread over rolled-out dough.

Roll up jellyroll fashion and place in a greased pan. Let rise about half an hour. Prick with a knitting needle to prevent the dough from forming blisters. Bake 40 minutes at 325° or till nicely browned. Brush with a little fruit juice or egg yolk and return to oven for 3 minutes. When cool, slice diagonally into half-inch sections or cookies. Place on greased cookie sheets and return to top shelf of oven to brown lightly, or toast under broiler flame for 2 minutes.

Yields about 21.

POPPYSEED ROLL (Yeast Dough)

2½ cups sifted all-purpose flour
½ teaspoon salt
½ package granular yeast
1 tablespoon sugar
⅔ cup lukewarm milk or milk and water

⅔ cup vegetable shortening or butter, softened
¼ cup sugar
grated rind and juice of 1 lemon
1 egg yolk

Sift together flour and salt in a deep mixing bowl. Dissolve yeast and sugar in the lukewarm liquid—a mixture of fruit juice and lukewarm water may be substituted for the milk or milk mixture. Cut in softened shortening. Add sugar, grated rind and juice to the flour, using a wire pastry blender or fingers. Stir in the yeast mixture as soon as it begins to bubble and knead well on a lightly floured pastry cloth or board. Cover with a towel and let rise at room temperature about 1 hour. Cut dough in two parts and roll out each into a rectangle about ¼-inch thick —thinner if possible.

Filling

1½ cups fine poppyseeds or ground coarse seeds
½ cup finely chopped seeded raisins or nuts

1 scant cup sugar
½ cup milk or fruit juice
3 tablespoons fine crumbs

Combine and cook in top of double boiler over boiling water till thick enough to spread with a spoon or spatula.

Spread with the filling and roll up jellyroll fashion.

Place in a greased baking pan, brush with diluted egg yolk and let rise in the pan about 30 minutes. Again brush top with egg yolk, prick with tines of a fork or a knitting needle to prevent blistering and bake 45 minutes at 325° or till lightly browned. Cool before slicing each roll into 10 or 12 diagonal cuts.

Variation: For Nut Roll, substitute ground almonds or walnuts for poppyseeds; chopped mixed candied fruits for raisins.

POPPYSEED TAYGLACH, Hungarian Style

2 cups sifted all-purpose flour	6 egg yolks
½ package granular yeast	¼ cup finely chopped almonds or
2 tablespoons lukewarm water	walnuts
¼ cup sugar	½ teaspoon vanilla or rum
¼ cup softened butter or substitute	¼ cup melted butter or substitute
½ teaspoon salt	½ cup poppyseeds
⅔ cup lukewarm milk	½ cup sugar

Sift flour into a large mixing bowl and make a well in the center. Dissolve yeast in lukewarm water, stir in sugar, softened butter or substitute, salt and milk till blended. Stir this mixture into the flour till about half the flour is blended in, then add egg yolks one at a time, stirring to blend till all the flour has been absorbed. Add the chopped nuts and flavoring and mix the batter till it forms a dough stiff enough to drop heavily from a spoon. It should be left at room temperature for 2 hours or till about double in bulk.

Pinch off balls of dough the size of hazelnuts, roll each in flour and place them about an inch apart each way on a lightly greased cookie sheet. Let rise 30 minutes and bake 50 minutes at 250° or till lightly browned. Remove these Tayglach to a deep bowl or sauce pan and cover with boiling water which should be poured off quickly—just a rinsing process. Have the melted butter or substitute in a heated frying pan large enough to hold them without crowding and turn the rinsed Tayglach in, stirring till coated with the fat. Sprinkle them with combined poppyseeds and sugar and stir till each is covered. Or turn the buttered Tayglach into a mixing bowl in which you have mixed the poppyseeds and sugar and stir or shake to achieve well-covered Tayglach.

Yields 48 to 50.

LITTLE DUTCH HAMANS

⅓ cup shortening	1 teaspoon each ground ginger,
1 cup dark brown sugar	allspice
1½ cups molasses	¼ teaspoon each cloves, cinnamon
½ cup water	and nutmeg
7 cups sifted flour	2 teaspoons baking soda
1 tablespoon salt	3 tablespoons water

Combine shortening, brown sugar and molasses, then stir in cold water till smooth. Sift together all dry ingredients except baking soda. Combine baking soda and water till it fizzes, and stir into the first mixture, adding the sifted dry ingredients gradually while mixing to a firm dough. Chill dough in refrigerator at least an hour. Roll out only as much at a time as can be handled easily and keep the rest in the refrigerator till needed.

Roll dough to ¼-inch thickness and use a gingerbread man cutter, or form dough into little gingerbread men about 3 inches tall. Place the Little Hamans on a well-greased cookie sheet an inch apart each way. Bake 18 to 20 minutes at 350° or till lightly browned. When cold, decorate with the following frosting.

Frosting

Mix confectioners' sugar with water to make a thin enough paste to spread lightly over the baked cakes. Make all white or tint some frosting with a drop of red vegetable coloring. Press raisins (or currants) down the front for buttons, or use red cinnamon candies for front and shoe buttons. Tips of Brazil nuts make nice shoes. Make the eyes of currants or bits of raisin and place a bit of slivered almond over each eye.

Yield depends on thickness and size of the Little Hamans.

PESACH OR PASSOVER, FESTIVAL OF FREEDOM

Many customs of a people grow from generation to generation, and acquire special significance in their reinterpretation from time to time. In an age of freedom from repressions of any kind, the aspects of the celebration that accentuate the spirit of liberty are given special importance in the reading or telling of the story of Passover as written in the Haggadah.

During the festive ritual of the *Seder,* for instance, each of the symbols, from the goblets of wine to the *Afikomen,* the *Bitter Herbs* and the *Charoses,* the *Bread of Affliction* (Matzo) to the chanting of the *Hallel* (Hallelujah), is explained so that even the youngest children may understand. The four cups of wine are likened to the Four Freedoms of our own day. The fifth cup has been suggested as a modern-day addition to the Seder Service in honor of the State of Israel and its first President, Dr. Chaim Weitzman. The return of the exiles to their ancient homeland acquires a new meaning in connection with the ancient story of the flight from Egypt. The open door, toward the end of the Service, is reinterpreted as not only an ever-welcome to Elijah, prophet and promise of hope and redemption, but a welcome to all the world to know and see this ancient ceremonial.

For the many Jews who gather together for a public Seder in Synagogue or Temple Community Centers, or in commodious hotel dining rooms, there is also a modern explanation. It is a home ceremonial away from home, inclusive of the "stranger within the gates." For in large cities especially, dining rooms in modest homes become too small for hospitality extended during the Passover Holidays. There are those without families, as well as men and women in the service of our country, to be invited as guests. For Passover is the season of remembrance as well as redemption from bondage, and Jewish hospitality plays its role magnificently.

The Seder Service also includes the singing of traditional songs like *Had Gadyu.* Other significant parts are the telling of the story of The Four Sons, each son symbolic of a characteristic of the people; the recitation of "The Litany of Wonders," from the marking of the doorposts that the Angel of Death may "skip over" those dwellings, to the parting of the Red Sea that the Israelites might safely pass before being overtaken by pursuing Egyptians. The "four questions" asked by the youngest child present serve as guideposts as well as logical reasons for participation of the children. The "stealing" of the *Afikomen* is also part of the service. Not only is continued interest maintained in the lengthy ritual, but children of all ages are thus included in the ceremonials of the *Seder*.

To quote Dr. Theodor H. Gaster*, "properly understood, the Seder ceremony is no mere act of pious recollection, but a unique and inspired device for blending the past, the present and the future into a single comprehensive and transcendental experience."

SEDER SYMBOLS

The Afikomen: Place three whole matzos in the folds of a napkin. These represent the traditional Sabbath or holiday loaves over which the benediction is pronounced.

A part of the *Afikomen* is spirited away during the Seder service and hidden for the younger set to find and present for redemption, some prize or coin.

Roast lamb bone: This is the symbol of an ancient custom of sacrifice brought to the Temple by each family. A chicken bone, roasted against the open flame, may serve as a substitute for a lamb bone.

Hard-cooked egg, roasted: The egg symbolizes life, the perpetuation of existence, eternal life. Place the hard-cooked egg in the shell against an open flame to roast on one side.

Bitter herbs—Morar: Place the top of a horseradish root, with green leaves, on the Seder Plate to symbolize the bitterness of Israel's bondage in the Land of Egypt. The *Morar* is made of grated horseradish, unflavored and unseasoned. During the service some of the *Morar* is placed between two small pieces of matzo and passed to each person around the festive board. This is referred to as "the Hillel Sandwich."

Charoses: Moisten chopped nuts and grated apple with wine and flavor with cinnamon. Addition of sugar to taste adds to the sweetness it represents in lightening the burdens of unhappy memory.

Hard-cooked egg and salt water: Sliced or diced hard-cooked eggs are placed in one dish or compartment of the Seder Plate and salt water in another. These are served to each during the service, added symbols of life's burdens and the hope of overcoming them, just as the parting of the Red Sea opened the way to freedom in the oft-told story of Passover.

Greens and salt water: Parsley, watercress, chicory, lettuce or other available greens are the symbols of hope and redemption. The greens are dipped in the salt water during the Service.

Wine: Specially prepared wine for Passover is served in goblets that are refilled four times during the Seder Service. This symbolizes the four-

* *Festivals of the Jewish Year,* by Theodor H. Gaster (Sloane Associates).

fold promise of redemption. Israel's statehood has suggested the refilling of the "fifth goblet," as mentioned above.

Cup of Elijah: A special goblet of wine is placed on the table toward the end of the Service and the door is opened and left ajar for "the coming of Elijah," symbolizing the hope for a more perfect world of justice and joy for all mankind.

TRADITIONAL PASSOVER FOODS

During the week of Passover, meals vary from those of the rest of the year. All vegetables, except those of the peas and beans family, are used by the most observant. Because legumes customarily are soaked before planting, these are forbidden for Passover use. No leavening agents such as yeast, baking powder and baking soda are permitted. The customary leavened bread is replaced by matzos and matzo meal, potato flour and matzo meal cake flour (finely ground matzo meal) and dishes made of these.

Meats and poultry as well as fish are permitted foods. No flour is used with these in the roasting or cooking.

Fresh fruits of all kinds, as well as canned or quick-frozen fruits and berries, are specially prepared and labeled "for Passover use." Wines and liquors, bottled drinks, such as gingerale and soda are also available with the above label.

Dairy products and shortenings, such as schmaltz and pareve fats are likewise marked "for Passover use."

Passover sweetmeats and chocolate are on the market.

Passover menus, omitting forbidden items, may be as varied and attractive as well as nutritionally adequate as family requirements and budget dictate. The culinary ingenuity of the kitchen engineer permits a wide latitude in the preparation and serving of meals during the week of Passover.

Suggested Menus for the Seder

MENU 1
*Gefilte Fish with Beet-Flavored
Horseradish
Chopped Liver on Lettuce or in
Pepper Rings
Chicken Soup with Knaidlach
Roast Chicken with Matzo-Prune
Dressing
Mixed Greens Salad
Passover Nut Cake
Tea with Orange or Lemon Slices*

MENU 2
*Gefilte Fish with Horseradish
Chicken Soup with Featherlight
Knaidlach
Roast Chicken with Matzo-
Farfel Dressing
Carrots in Lemon Sauce
Tomato and Green Pepper Salad
Stewed Rhubarb and Strawberries
Passover Sponge Cake
Tea with Marmalade*

MENU 3
*Gefilte Fish Balls on Lettuce
Chopped Liver in Celery Sticks
Roast Turkey with Matzo-
Prune Dressing
Cauliflower with Parsley Garnish
Mixed Greens Salad with
Passover Dressing
Passover Komishbrodt
Tea with Lemon Slices*

MENU 4
*Gefilte Fish with Horseradish
Chopped Liver on Lettuce
Chicken Soup with Knaidlach
Broiled Chicken with Browned
Potatoes
Passover Beet Preserves
Greens Salad with Passover
Dressing
Passover Sponge Cake
Tea, Black Coffee or Mead*

Suggested Menus for Passover Breakfasts

MENU 1
*Grapefruit with Honey
Eggs, Boiled, Poached or Fried
Matzo Meal Muffins
Butter, Jam or Preserves
Coffee, Tea, Milk*

MENU 2
*Fruit Juice
Matzo Brie
Stewed Fresh or Dried Fruit
Beverage*

MENU 3
*Sliced Bananas with Milk
Matzo Meal Pancakes with
Preserves
Sour Cream and Cheese
Beverage*

MENU 4
*Stewed Prunes or Other
Dried Fruit
Multi-Layer Pancakes
Beverage*

Suggested Menus for Passover Luncheons

Menu 1
Fruit Cup
Baked, Broiled or Fried Fish
Pickled Beet Relish
Matzo Meal Muffins
Raw Carrot Salad
Beverage
Macaroons

Menu 2
Broiled Grapefruit Halves
Creamed Eggs on Fried Matzos
Carrot Curls, Celery, Pickled
Peppers
Beverage
Matzo Farfel Pudding

Menu 3
Beet or Spinach Borscht
with Sour Cream
Boiled Potatoes or Diced Eggs
Cottage Cheese in Green Pepper
Boats, Sour Cream Dressing
Shredded Cabbage and Carrots
Passover Cake or Cookies
Beverage

Menu 4
Fruit Juice
Passover Scrambled Eggs
Tossed Greens Salad, Dressing
Fried Matzo
Passover Komishbrodt
Beverage

Suggested Menus for Passover Dinners

Menu 1
Fruit Cup
Passover Carnatzlach
Tomato Sauce
Grated Potato Kugelach
Tossed Greens Salad, Dressing
Passover Nut Cake
Beverage

Menu 2
Vegetable Soup
Meat-Filled Latkes
Cauliflower, Matzo Meal Topping
Tomato and Cucumber Salad
Passover Sponge Cake,
Fresh Berries
Beverage

Menu 3
Clear Beef Broth with Tiny
Drop Knaidlach
Boiled Beef with Horseradish
Sunburst Salad
Almond Macaroons
Beverage

Menu 4
Broiled Grapefruit Halves
Oven-Broiled Chickens
Grated Potato Pancakes
Grated Cabbage and Apple
on Lettuce
Stewed Fruit, Cookies
Beverage

Milchig Passover Dinners

MENU 5	MENU 6
Stewed Prunes	Beet Borscht, Hot or Iced with
Sweet-Sour Fish	Diced Cucumber Garnish
Baked Potatoes	Baked Gefilte Fish
Beets with Orange Sauce	Butter and Parsley Sauce
Mixed Greens Salad,	Mashed Potatoes
French Dressing	Eggplant with Tomato Sauce
Matzo Meal Muffins	Chremzlach with Stewed Rhubarb
Hot or Cold Beverage	and Strawberries
	Coffee, Tea or Milk

MEAD FOR PASSOVER

2 gallons strained honey
8 gallons water
2 ounces dry hops (from drug-
　store)

2 lemons, sliced very thin
1½ ounces ginger root (from drug-
　store)

Cook honey and water, in a large vessel, up to the boiling point, then
add the hops, tied in a square of cheesecloth or muslin, lemon slices and
ginger root. Reduce heat to a simmer and cook 30 minutes. Skim during
the cooking process as frequently as necessary. Let Mead cool in the
cooking vessel before straining through a double layer of fine cheesecloth
into a 10-gallon wooden cask. The cask should not be filled more than
two-thirds full to permit fermentation without overflow. Be sure the cask
remains uncorked but covered, at room temperature until fermentation
stops, approximately three weeks.

Before drawing off, carmelize 1 cup of sugar over moderate heat till
it becomes deep golden in color. Add a little of the Mead, stirring in till
smooth. Add to the Mead only after fermentation has stopped. It pro-
duces that deep amber color of Mead which makes it delightful to the
eye as well as to the palate.

The Mead may be left in the cask and drawn off as needed, or drawn
into bottles which should be corked securely before storing in a dark
place at approximately room temperature—68° to 70°. It may be iced
one or two hours before serving time if desired.

Yields approximately 8 gallons.

HOMEMADE PASSOVER WINE

With excellent wines for Passover use imported from Israel, and fine
wines produced in this country, the modern home-maker generally does
not resort to the homemade wines of Grandmother's day. However, in
sections of the country where Damson plums are plentiful, some still
make Damson Plum Wine for Passover.

The following recipe has been handed down for several generations
in the family of the writer and evokes happy memories of this special
treat for Passover Week. Here is the way to make

DAMSON PLUM WINE

10 gallons Damson plums
　(approximately 80 pounds)

10 gallons boiling water
2½ pounds sugar per gallon
　strained juice

Remove stems from plums. Rinse in running cold water and drain well. With a knitting needle pierce each plum in one or two places and put plums into a 15-gallon cask or barrel with a bung and cork. Add the boiling water slowly. Let stand uncorked for 48 hours at room temperature. Draw off the juice through the faucet of barrel into large containers. Measure and add sugar as directed above. Stir till sugar is melted. Return to barrel and cover the bunghole with several thicknesses of cheesecloth or muslin. Let stand till fermentation has stopped. Remove the cheesecloth or muslin and adjust the cork or bung. Let stand from the time of straining till Passover and draw off as required into pitchers or bottles. Or draw off just before Passover into bottles, cork and store in a moderately cool place away from light. The wine should be rich in color and bouquet.

The Damson plums left in the barrel after draining off wine may be utilized for making preserves or may be eaten plain. They are plums with a brandy flavor and make good additions to fruit salads and other garnishes.

Variation: Add 1 quart good Passover brandy to strained wine.

CHAROSES

6 tart apples, cored, grated	1 teaspoon cinnamon
2 cups shelled, blanched almonds, ground or chopped	1 teaspoon ground ginger
	grated rind of 1 lemon or orange
¼ cup walnut meats, ground or chopped	3 or 4 tablespoons juice of lemon or orange
3 tablespoons sugar or honey	Passover wine to make mixture right consistency

Combine thoroughly to make a tasty mixture, thick enough to keep its shape when served on pieces of matzo at the Seder.
Serves 10 to 15.

PASSOVER GEFILTE FISH

2 pounds carp, filleted	2 stalks celery with leaves, diced
1 pound white fish, yellow pike or flounder, filleted	1 large carrot, thinly sliced
	1 large onion, thinly sliced
1 onion, grated	bones, skin, head (eyes and gills removed)
1 carrot, grated	
3 eggs	1 matzo, soaked in cold water and pressed dry
1 tablespoon salt	

Combine the fish and put through grinder twice. Add grated onion and carrot, eggs and half the amount of salt listed. Mix well. Form a nest in the bottom of a large cooking pot of diced celery, carrot slices, sliced

onion. Add washed and drained fish bones, skin and head. Now work the
soaked matzo well into the fish mixture and form into balls. Place the
balls on the nest of bones and vegetables, add cold water to cover and
bring to a boil. Reduce heat to a mild simmer, adding the remaining salt
to the liquid. Shaking pot to distribute it is a good way to do this. Cover
partly to permit steam to escape. Let simmer 1½ to 2 hours, or till the
liquid has been reduced by half. Let cool before lifting out cooked fish
balls to a platter. Strain the sauce over fish balls or into a separate dish.
Chill till ready to serve. If sauce is to be served separately, it may be cut
into squares when jelled.

Cooking Gefilte Fish the day before using is a good rule.

Serves 8 to 10.

SOUP ACCOMPANIMENTS AND GARNISHES

TOASTED FARFEL

1½ cups matzo farfel	½ teaspoon salt
2 eggs	3 tablespoons schmaltz

Combine listed ingredients, mixing well to distribute egg evenly.
Spread in an even thin layer over bottom of shallow baking pan. Bake at
400° for 8 to 10 minutes or till lightly browned. Or slip under broiler
flame to toast till lightly browned on top. Stir to expose untoasted bits
till lightly browned. Add to clear soup at table.

Serves 6.

FEATHERWEIGHT KNAIDLACH

2 eggs	⅓ to ½ cup cold water
4 tablespoons schmaltz	1 teaspoon salt
1 cup matzo meal	a dash of nutmeg or cinnamon (optional)

Beat eggs lightly and stir in the listed ingredients to form a stiff
batter. Cover and chill in refrigerator at least two hours. About a half
hour before serving time, form the batter into Knaidlach (little balls)
and drop into rapidly boiling salted water. Cover and cook 30 minutes.
Drain and serve in hot clear soup.

Serves 4.

FAT-FREE KNAIDLACH

⅓ cup matzo meal	⅓ cup matzo meal
½ teaspoon salt	2 eggs, separated
⅓ cup gingerale or plain soda	1 tablespoon minced parsley

Combine the first three ingredients listed into a smooth paste and chill 1 hour in the refrigerator. Add matzo meal and stir in egg yolks and minced parsley. Beat egg whites at room temperature till stiff but not dry and fold in. Chill 2 hours in the refrigerator. Form into balls about an inch in diameter and drop into rapidly boiling salted water. Cover and cook at moderate heat 30 minutes. Drain or skim out with a perforated spoon. Add to hot clear soup. May be served with hot milk.

Yields 24 small Knaidlach, 6 servings.

TINY DROP KNAIDLACH (Fat-free)

2 eggs	1 scant cup matzo meal
1/8 teaspoon salt	a dash of ginger or minced parsley

Beat eggs and salt till creamy. Stir in matzo meal and ginger or minced parsley to make a thick batter. Refrigerate for 1 hour. Drop from the tip of a teaspoon into rapidly boiling clear soup or salted water and cook 10 minutes or till Knaidlach rise to the top. Skim out of salted water and add to hot clear soup.

Yields 24 to 30.

GRANNY'S KNAIDLACH (Basic Recipe)

2 eggs, separated	1/2 teaspoon salt
1/2 cup matzo meal	

Beat egg whites and yolks separately. Stir matzo meal into beaten egg yolks till smooth. Add salt and stiffly beaten egg whites with a foldover motion. Do not beat. Refrigerate 30 minutes. Form into small balls, not more than one inch in diameter, by rolling lightly in greased palms. Drop into rapidly boiling clear soup or salted water. Cover and cook at a slow boil for 20 minutes. Knaidlach should double in size and rise to the top. Skim out of salted water and add to hot clear soup just before serving time.

Serves 3 to 4.

Variation 1: For added zest, add a dash of ground ginger to the mixture.

Variation 2: Combine the mixture with 2 tablespoons chopped chicken liver and a few bits of parsley. Form into balls or drop from tip of teaspoon into slowly boiling clear soup. Cook as above.

Variation 3: Add 1 tablespoon cooked or uncooked marrow from beef shinbone and mix thoroughly before forming into balls and cooking.

SOUP MANDLEN FOR PASSOVER

3 eggs
1/8 teaspoon salt
2/3 cup matzo cake flour

1/2 teaspoon potato flour
hot melted shortening for deep
  frying

Beat eggs and add the other ingredients in the order listed. Let stand 5 to 10 minutes. Drop from the tip of a teaspoon into deep, hot melted shortening and let cook until nicely browned. Skim out with a perforated spoon and drain off excess fat on paper towels. These can be made in advance and stored in a paper bag until wanted to serve with clear soup. Reheat in the paper bag in the oven at 375° 3 to 5 minutes.

Serves 4 to 6.

Variation: Add 1/3 cup matzo cake flour and 1 tablespoon finely ground almonds to the batter as in basic recipe. Turn out onto a board dusted with more matzo cake flour and pat or roll out to 1/2-inch thickness. Cut into strips 1/2-inch wide and roll each strip with the palms of the hands. With a sharp knife cut each roll into 1/4-inch pieces and drop them into deep hot melted shortening for frying until light brown.

MATZO MEAL SOUPLETS

1 cup boiling water
1/2 cup schmaltz or substitute

1/4 teaspoon salt
3/4 cup matzo meal
4 eggs

Bring water and schmaltz to a boil, preferably in the top of a double boiler. Combine salt and matzo meal and dump into the liquid all at once, stirring till a ball of dough is formed that stands away from sides of pan. Let cool 5 to 10 minutes. Beat in one egg at a time. Drop from the tip of a teaspoon onto a lightly greased cookie sheet and bake 10 minutes at 400°, then turn down heat to 375° for 10 to 15 minutes or till lightly browned. These may be stored for later serving with clear soup.

Yields 36 to 40, depending on size of drops.

MATZO DRESSING FOR POULTRY (Basic Recipe)

4 matzos, broken
cold water to cover
3 eggs
1 teaspoon salt

3 tablespoons schmaltz
1 onion, finely diced
1/2 cup finely diced celery
1 green pepper, diced

Break matzos into cold water in a deep bowl and let stand 5 minutes. Squeeze dry and return to mixing bowl. Beat eggs with salt till creamy and stir into moist matzos. Melt schmaltz and add diced onion, cooking over moderate heat till lightly browned. Add celery and green pepper, stir 1 minute and add to the other mixture.

Yields enough stuffing for an average-size fowl.

Variation 1: Omit celery and green pepper. Add 1 cup finely cut dried prunes and 3 tablespoons sugar. Season with ¼ teaspoon cinnamon or a little grated lemon rind.

Variation 2: Substitute ½ cup finely cut roasted chestnuts for the celery and ½ cup raisins for the green pepper. Add 3 tablespoons sugar and a dash of nutmeg.

Variation 3: 8 to 12 prunes, pitted after soaking, may be substituted for vegetables, except fried onion, in basic recipe. Add 3 tablespoons sugar and a dash of cinnamon.

MATZO FARFEL DRESSING

3½ cups matzo farfel (dried matzo may be crumbled)
½ cup cold water
1 teaspoon salt
3 eggs

4 tablespoons melted shortening (schmaltz)
1 onion, diced fine
1 cup finely cut dried prunes
2 tablespoons sugar
a dash of cinnamon

Sprinkle the matzo farfel with cold water. Beat eggs in a mixing bowl and stir in the moistened farfel and salt. Lightly brown diced onion in hot fat and turn this into the mixture while hot. Stir with two forks and let cool before adding the prunes, sugar and cinnamon. Return the mixture to frying pan and stir while over moderate heat until excess moisture has been eliminated, or you will have a moist, heavy dressing. Let cool before filling chicken in the customary manner.

For a 4½ to 5 pound chicken.

MIXED POTATO DRESSING FOR POULTRY

2 cups cooked, mashed white potatoes
2 cups cooked, mashed sweet potatoes

1 tablespoon grated orange rind
½ cup matzo meal
2 eggs, beaten slightly and folded in last

Combine ingredients in the order listed as soon as potatoes are cool. Stuff into cavity of chicken and close the opening by drawing the skin together and fastening with toothpicks.

Sufficient for 4½ to 5½ pound chicken.

MATZO-PRUNE STUFFING FOR TURKEY

14 matzos, broken into small pieces
  cold water to cover
  turkey giblets, cut fine and boiled
  tender
⅛ teaspoon salt
  parsley
  a few slices carrot
  slice of onion
12 large prunes, soaked, pitted
  and cut fine

4 tablespoons schmaltz (or vegetable shortening)
1 large onion, diced fine
4 eggs, separated
1 tablespoon salt
2 tablespoons sugar
¼ teaspoon cinnamon, ginger or nutmeg
½ cup soup stock (from boiled giblets)

Soak broken matzo in cold water till soft. Squeeze dry and place in a large mixing bowl. Put the cut giblets in cold water to cover, add salt, parsley, sliced carrot and slice of onion, and cook over low heat till tender, approximately 20 minutes. Drain and save the stock for later use in dressing. Cut up soaked and pitted prunes. Combine cooked giblets and cooked carrot slices with prepared prunes and mix with the prepared matzo in bowl. Melt schmaltz in a large frying pan over moderate heat and lightly brown the diced onion, stirring frequently. Add the matzo mixture and stir well over moderate heat till the onions are well mixed into the other ingredients and the under side turns light brown and becomes slightly dry. Turn or break up in the pan to achieve the lightly browned effect for the rest of pan contents.

Let cool before adding beaten egg yolks, salt, sugar and spice. Stir well, adding the stock gradually to moisten. Beat egg whites and fold into the mixture. If any stuffing is left after filling the prepared turkey, form into balls and place around the roasting turkey after it begins to brown. The balls should be nicely browned by the time the stuffed turkey is done and ready to serve, and the crusted stuffing balls are most attractive as additional garnish.

Sufficient for a 16 to 18 pound turkey.

Variation: Omit prunes and substitute same amount of shredded or diced tart apple sprinkled with some lemon juice.

VEGETABLE DISHES FOR PASSOVER

All vegetables except legumes, those of the peas and beans family, are permitted during the week of Passover. Peas and beans must be soaked before planting. Traditional prohibitions forbid their use for Passover because the soaking may have been done in non-Passover vessels.

Be sure to inspect canned or frozen vegetables for the Passover label or mark of acceptance for such use.

CAULIFLOWER, MATZO MEAL TOPPING

Soak cauliflower in salted water, head down, for 10 minutes. Rinse under running cold water. If it is to be served whole, cover with cold water, add ½ teaspoon salt and 1 teaspoon lemon juice. Cover and cook till it begins to boil. Uncover and cook 15 to 20 minutes or till tender enough to pierce with the tines of a fork. Drain well. Top with the following basic mixture.

3 tablespoons butter or peanut oil (schmaltz if for meat dinner)

3 tablespoons matzo meal
a dash of pepper or paprika

Brown the matzo meal in hot melted shortening used over moderate heat in a small frying pan or saucepan. Season to taste. Sprinkle on top of cooked cauliflower just before serving time.

An average head of cauliflower will serve 4.

EGGPLANT WITH TOMATO SAUCE

1 to 1½ pounds eggplant
1 teaspoon salt
4 tablespoons matzo meal
1 large onion, diced or sliced

1 cup thick tomato sauce
1 tablespoon sugar
1 tablespoon lemon juice
2 tablespoons peanut oil

Pare and dice eggplant into 1-inch cubes. Combine salt and matzo meal by sifting together through a soup strainer over the cubed eggplant and prepared onion, stirring to coat well, if necessary. Add the other ingredients listed and cook over moderate heat in a covered saucepan for 8 to 10 minutes. The moisture from the vegetables plus tomato sauce and lemon juice should be sufficient liquid. Hot water may be added, a tablespoon at a time, if the mixture should thicken before the onion and eggplant are tender. Serve hot.

Serves 4 to 6.

MATZO FARFEL AND MUSHROOMS

2 cups matzo farfel (matzo crumbles)
1 quart boiling water
3 eggs, separated

1 large onion, diced
4 tablespoons schmaltz
½ pound fresh mushrooms, sliced
2 tablespoons matzo meal
1 teaspoon salt

Place the matzo farfel (or crumbles) in a strainer and pour boiling water over slowly. Drain well. Beat egg yolks and add drained farfel, stirring well. Brown diced onion in hot schmaltz or other shortening, add sliced fresh mushrooms and matzo meal, stirring well. Turn in the farfel mixture, adding salt and stirring over moderate heat for 3 minutes. Beat egg whites and fold into the warm mixture in frying pan. Turn off heat. Turn the mixture into a greased pudding dish or casserole and bake 30 minutes at 350° or till browned on top. Serve hot, with meat, poultry or fish dishes.

Serves 8.

STUFFED GREEN PEPPER HALVES

4 large bell peppers, red or green	2 tablespoons melted fat or
3 matzos	peanut oil
3 eggs	1 diced onion
3 tablespoons cold water	1 teaspoon salt

Wash and cut peppers lengthwise from stem to blossom end. Remove seeds. Break matzos into small bits in a mixing bowl. Beat eggs slightly, adding cold water till combined. Turn over the broken matzos and let stand while browning the diced onion in hot melted fat. Combine with the soaked matzos, mixing well. Add salt to taste. Stuff each pepper half, pressing the filling in firmly and rounding up on top. Brush tops with a little shortening and bake in pan covered with aluminum foil for 10 minutes at 375°. Remove foil to brown tops for 5 to 10 minutes at the same temperature. If peppers are not tender, leave aluminum foil cover on for 5 minutes longer before removing. May also be browned under broiler flame just before serving time.

Serves 8 as a vegetable with main dish.

Variation 1: Add ½ cup finely chopped leftover chicken or meat of any kind. Mix well.

Variation 2: Fill pepper halves with fish salad made by combining

2 cups flaked leftover fish—baked, broiled or boiled	1 cup chopped celery
	¼ cup finely cut green onions
4 hard-cooked eggs, chopped	¼ cup Passover Salad Dressing

BAKED ACORN SQUASH (Basic Recipe)

3 acorn squash, average size	¼ teaspoon salt
2 tablespoons melted shortening	

Cut the acorn squash in halves from stem to blossom end and remove seeds and fibers. Combine melted shortening with salt and sprinkle or brush insides of each squash half. Bake on a cookie sheet 30 to 35 minutes at 375° or till the squash is tender enough to pierce with a toothpick. Serve plain or with any of the following modifications or variations.

Serves 6.

Variation 1: For meat or fish meals, fill centers with cooked rice mixed with browned onion, green pepper, celery and one egg per cup of the mixture. Season to suit the taste—pepper, paprika or your favorite herb seasoning. Heap the filling into the cavities and slip under broiler flame to brown lightly before serving.

Variation 2: With poultry of any kind, fill the cavity of each squash half with applesauce to which has been added 1 teaspoon lemon juice per cupful, 2 tablespoons raisins (seeded or seedless), 1 tablespoon brown sugar. Return to oven for 10 minutes or until the filling has been heated through, then slip under broiler flame to brown lightly. Top with a little raspberry or cherry preserves for color and glamour.

Variation 3: Fill baked halves with chopped meat, seasoned with salt, pepper, paprika, grated onion or onion salt. Heat uncooked chopped meat and seasoning in a frying pan, stirring till lightly browned. Add one egg per pound and heap into squash cavities. Serve hot.

VEGETABLE PATTIES

1 cup cooked green pepper chopped fine	1 tablespoon grated raw onion
	1 tablespoon minced parsley
1 cup grated raw carrot, tightly packed	3 eggs
	1 teaspoon salt
1 cup raw spinach, chopped, tightly packed	a dash of pepper
	1 cup matzo meal
2 medium-size potatoes, boiled and mashed	melted fat or vegetable shortening for frying

Combine all vegetables in a mixing bowl and add eggs, one at a time, mixing well after each addition. Season to taste with salt and pepper. Stir in matzo meal and let stand 30 minutes in the refrigerator. Form into patties 2½ inches in diameter and fry in hot melted chicken or goose schmaltz for meat meals, or use Passover all-purpose shortening or oil. Be sure to brown on under side before turning to brown well. Drain on paper towels. Serve hot.

Serves 6 to 8.

PASSOVER BAGEL

⅔ cup water	1 scant cup matzo meal
⅓ cup butter or all-purpose shortening	⅔ teaspoon salt
	1 tablespoon sugar
	3 eggs

Heat water and butter or other shortening in a saucepan, stirring well to combine. This liquid need not be brought to boiling point. Stir in

matzo meal, salt and sugar and continue stirring till all the liquid has
been absorbed. Be sure to keep the saucepan over low heat during the
stirring period. Remove from heat and add one egg at a time, stirring and
beating well after each addition. The batter should be heavy enough to
drop from a tablespoon and hold its shape. Grease a cookie sheet and
drop the batter several inches apart on the prepared cookie sheet. With
the point of the spoon, make a hole in each, shaping like doughnuts.
Bake 40 minutes at 375° or till nicely browned. Brush lightly with a little
sugar and water for glaze and return for 3 minutes to oven.

Yields 8 to 12, depending on size.

MATZO MEAL MUFFINS (Basic Recipe)

3 eggs	1½ cups matzo meal
½ teaspoon salt	4 tablespoons melted shortening
1 cup water	a little grated lemon or orange rind

Beat eggs in a mixing bowl. Add salt, water and matzo meal, stirring
till a thick batter is formed. Heat shortening to be used—either neutral
(pareve) or schmaltz. Grease muffin pans well and stir the hot fat into the
batter till well blended. Fill 8 large or 16 small muffin rings two-thirds
full and bake 30 minutes at 350° or till lightly browned.

Yields 8 large or 16 small muffins.

MATZO MEAL ROLLS

1 cup water	2 tablespoons sugar
½ cup shortening	1 cup matzo meal
2 teaspoons salt	4 eggs

Bring water to a quick boil in a double boiler and add shortening,
salt and sugar. Stir in matzo meal quickly and beat with a fork while
keeping the water in the lower part of double boiler over moderate heat.
The mixture should form a ball of heavy batter in a few minutes. Remove
from heat. Add one egg at a time, beating well after each addition. Drop
from a tablespoon and shape with bowl of spoon to form 2½-inch rolls.
Use a greased baking sheet or a shallow pan. Bake 30 minutes at 350°;
mark tops of rolls with the point of a paring knife in any desired design
and continue baking 10 minutes or till nicely browned and crusted.

Yields 8 to 10.

MATZO MEAL CHEESE KNAIDLACH

½ pound cottage cheese (dry kind)	a pinch of salt
2 eggs, separated	4 to 5 tablespoons matzo meal
2 tablespoons sugar	2 tablespoons melted butter

Press the cheese through a strainer into a bowl. Add egg yolks and sugar and mix well. Stir in matzo meal to make a batter thick enough to form into balls. Add melted butter, mixing well. Beat egg whites and fold in lightly. Let stand 30 minutes. Form into 1½-inch balls or Knaidlach and drop into rapidly boiling salted water, one at a time. Let cook 10 to 15 minutes at moderate heat. The Knaidlach will rise to top when done. Skim out. Dust with a mixture of cinnamon and sugar and top with sour cream or applesauce. Or serve with warm milk.

Serves 4.

CHEESE-MATZO PANCAKES

3 matzos, crumbled	3 eggs, separated
½ cup cottage cheese	a dash of cinnamon or nutmeg
½ teaspoon salt	2 tablespoons melted butter
3 tablespoons sugar	additional butter for frying

Combine crumbled matzos, cottage cheese, salt and sugar. Add egg yolks one at a time and mix well. Stir in cinnamon or nutmeg and 2 tablespoons melted butter. Grease a frying pan and drop the batter from a tablespoon on the hot frying pan over moderate heat. Fry till bottoms of pancakes are lightly browned before turning to brown the other side. Remove to a heated plate or platter and serve hot with sour cream, sugar and cinnamon, honey or any fruit sauce.

Serves 4.

CRISP MATZO MEAL PANCAKES (Basic Recipe)

3 eggs, separated	1 small onion, grated
½ cup cold water	1 tablespoon melted shortening
¼ teaspoon salt	melted shortening or oil for deep
1 cup matzo meal	frying

Beat egg yolks and stir in water, salt and matzo meal. Beat egg whites and fold in. Add grated onion and tablespoon of melted shortening, mixing to a smooth heavy batter. If batter is too thin to drop heavily from a spoon, add a tablespoon of matzo meal, stirring well. Heat the all-purpose shortening or oil in a heavy frying pan and drop the batter from a tablespoon to make pancakes about 2½ inches in diameter. Let cook in the shortening that should come almost to the top of the pancakes when the frying pan is filled. The pancakes should be turned with a fork or pancake turner to brown nicely on both sides. The pancakes should be crisp and light if cooked in this manner. Let drain on a double fold of paper napkins. If making a double recipe, keep pancakes warm in an uncovered pan in the oven at 325° till ready to serve.

Serves 4.

Variation 1: Omit grated onion if pancakes are to be served as a dessert with applesauce, cranberry sauce, dried fruit compote or honey. Add ¼ teaspoon grated lemon or orange rind and 1 tablespoon lemon or orange juice to the batter.

Variation 2: To serve with cheese and sour cream, substitute milk for the water in basic recipe. Grated onion is optional. Or top with cottage cheese and sour cream and sprinkle with minced green onions or scallions, and/or minced parsley.

CHREMZLACH (Basic Recipe)

3 tablespoons fat (chicken, goose or vegetable shortening)	4 cups matzo meal (approximately)
6 tablespoons hot water	4 eggs, separated
1 lemon, grated rind and juice	¼ teaspoon salt
	hot melted shortening for deep frying

Melt the shortening by adding hot water and stirring well. Add grated rind and lemon juice. Use a large mixing bowl. Stir in matzo meal gradually to make a stiff batter free of lumps. Beat egg yolks till creamy and stir into batter. Sugar may be added to the yolks while beating if desired, in any amount to suit the taste, but is not essential as the honey topping is generally sufficient. Beat egg whites with salt till stiff but not dry and fold in. Matzo meal varies in absorptive capacity, so be sure to have the batter stiff enough for molding into balls the size of medium apples. Greasing the palms of hands facilitates this procedure. After the balls are formed and placed on a platter, prepare one of the following fillings:

Filling No. 1

1½ cups fruit preserves (cherry preferred)	½ cup chopped almonds (or mixed nuts)
	2 tablespoons matzo meal

Combine well and let stand 10 minutes.

Filling No. 2

1½ cups grated tart apple, tightly packed	4 tablespoons sugar
½ cup finely chopped or ground almonds	½ teaspoon cinnamon
	a dash of nutmeg
	3 tablespoons matzo cake flour

Place a tablespoonful of the filling in the depression made in each ball of dough and tuck in, rolling in palm of hand till covered. Flatten each filled Chremzle into a thick pancake and fry in hot melted fat in a

heavy frying pan till lightly browned before turning to brown the other side. Lift out and drain on paper towels. When all have been fried, arrange on serving plate and cover with honey and slivered almonds. Or top with marmalade of your choice. Or dust with sugar. Serve hot or cold. To keep hot, leave in oven with door open after preheating to 375°.
Yields 20 to 24.

CHREMZLACH, BOSTON STYLE

6 eggs	3 tablespoons melted shortening
1½ cups matzo meal	(schmaltz, vegetable or oil)
6 tablespoons cold water	½ teaspoon salt

Beat eggs with a rotary beater 3 minutes. Stir in matzo meal and water alternately and add melted shortening and salt, stirring well to combine. Chill 2 hours in refrigerator. During this time prepare the filling:

Filling

¾ cup chopped rossel beets (or drained cooked beets)	¼ cup chopped almonds or mixed nuts
½ cup honey	¼ teaspoon ginger
	⅓ cup very strong tea

Combine ingredients except tea. Cook over moderate heat, stirring constantly till thick. Be careful not to scorch this mixture. Remove from heat and stir in tea. Let cool before using as filling.

After batter mixture has been chilled, form into 16 flat cakes about 2½ or 3 inches in diameter. Place 8 cakes on a well-greased cookie sheet or baking pan and drop a teaspoonful of filling mixture on each. Cover with the remaining 8 flat cakes and press the edges together with the tines of a fork, gently but firmly. Bake 20 minutes at 425° or till nicely browned. Dust with sugar and cinnamon, or top each baked Chremzle with a little of the filling used, which may be reserved or the quantity increased in the preparation of same.
Yields 8.

MATZO BRIE (Fried Matzos) (Basic Recipe)

1 egg for each matzo used	¼ cup water
	a dash of salt

Beat egg in a deep bowl, adding salt and water to dilute. Break matzo into bits, stir in and let stand 5 minutes to soften before frying in a heavy pan in which schmaltz or other shortening has been heated. If this is to be used as a garnish for soup or meat, additional flavor is achieved by frying finely diced onion in the hot fat before pouring in the mixture of egg and matzo. Cover and cook over moderate heat until lightly browned, then turn and brown under side, stirring a few times to break up the mass.

Breakfast Dish: To the fried matzos mixture, add 1 tablespoon honey and 2 tablespoons lemon or orange juice, then fry. Serve with milk, sour cream, cottage cheese or stewed fruit. Stewed rhubarb makes it yummy!

Luncheon Dish: Serve with little homemade sausages fried brown, and plenty of apple sauce. An attractive salad of any kind and a hot or cold beverage make it complete.

CREAMED EGGS ON FRIED MATZOS

3 eggs	3 tablespoons cold water
¼ teaspoon salt	2 matzos
	3 tablespoons melted butter or oil

Beat eggs and salt in a deep bowl till creamy. Use a rotary beater or fork. Add cold water, stirring well. Break matzos into small pieces and add to the mixture, stirring well. Let stand while preparing the eggs as directed below. When ready to serve, turn the matzos-egg mixture into hot melted butter or oil in a heavy frying pan. Cook over moderate heat 3 to 5 minutes, covered, then lift cover to permit steam to escape. Turn out on a heated serving plate and top with the eggs prepared as follows:

Creamed Eggs

4 hard-cooked eggs, sliced or diced	3 tablespoons melted butter
1 green pepper, diced fine and/or ½ cup each green onions, cut fine, and ¼ cup minced parsley	2 tablespoons matzo cake meal
	½ cup milk
	⅛ teaspoon each salt and paprika

Combine hard-cooked eggs with the greens. Stir matzo cake meal into hot melted butter or oil in a saucepan for 2 minutes or till lightly browned. Stir in milk gradually till the mixture begins to thicken. Add the eggs and greens combination and cook with the seasonings over low heat only till heated through, about 2 minutes. Stir lightly and turn out over the fried matzos. Serve hot with additional minced parsley, or chopped green pepper and/or green onion for garnish. Good for breakfast or luncheon main dish.

Serves 2 to 4.

PASSOVER OMELETTES (Basic Recipe)

6 eggs, separated	2 tablespoons melted butter or other fat
¼ teaspoon salt	
¼ cup matzo meal	1 tablespoon minced parsley

Beat egg yolks in a mixing bowl, using a rotary beater. In a separate bowl beat egg whites and salt at room temperature till stiff but not dry. Stir matzo meal into beaten yolks and fold in egg whites lightly. Heat shortening in a 9-inch frying pan, turn in the batter and cook over moderate heat, covered, 8 minutes. The omelette should be puffed to top of pan but not dry on top. Sprinkle minced parsley over top and quickly fold over the other half. Slip onto a warm serving platter and garnish with parsley. Serve at once.

Serves 4.

Variation: Top the omelette with cottage cheese and minced green onion, scallions and/or parsley before folding over.

PASSOVER SCRAMBLED EGGS (Basic Recipe)

8 eggs, separated
1 teaspoon salt
4 tablespoons matzo cake meal

2 tablespoons melted shortening (schmaltz, oil or vegetable shortening)

Beat yolks till light and creamy, using a rotary beater. Beat egg whites with salt till stiff but not dry. Fold into beaten yolks, alternately with matzo cake meal, as lightly as possible. Heat shortening in a heavy frying pan and turn in the mixture. Stir lightly as soon as the mixture begins to thicken, using a fork at center of frying pan and twirling it slowly to bring the scrambled eggs up to a peak as the mixture thickens. Be sure to keep heat moderate for best results. Serve on a heated serving plate, garnished with minced parsley, fried onion rings or bits of fresh green pepper for color contrast.

Serves 4.

Variation: Fold 2 tablespoons finely minced parsley into mixture before cooking. Needs no further garnish.

CHOPPED EGG SALAD

6 hard-cooked eggs, chopped or finely diced
1/8 teaspoon salt
a dash of paprika or celery salt
1 medium-size onion, chopped or finely diced

3 tablespoons chopped green pepper or minced parsley
3 tablespoons sour cream
2 tablespoons lemon juice
1/2 teaspoon sugar
1 egg yolk (optional)
a dash of salt and pepper

Combine in the order listed above. Chill 30 minutes. Serve in lettuce cups or on shredded salad greens with fish or meatless main dishes. Makes a good, nourishing luncheon dish served with Matzo Meal or Grated Potato Pancakes.

Serves 4.

Fleishig: Substitute equal amount of schmaltz for sour cream. The addition of chopped *greben* adds glamour and calories.

Pareve: Substitute equal amount of olive or vegetable oil for the sour cream, mixing oil, lemon juice, egg yolk and salt to form a dressing to be stirred in just before serving time.

Note: This is an excellent filling for tomatoes set on a bed of salad greens.

EGGS RUMANIAN

Preheat fat used and slip each whole egg from saucer into hot shortening in a heavy frying pan. Cook over low heat to prevent toughening of edges. Tilt the pan as soon as eggs begin to set or turn white and baste tops with some of the hot fat in pan till the yolks are coated with a white film. Cooking process should take about 5 minutes. *Do not overcook.* The yolks should remain soft under the white coating. Serve hot with a sprinkling of salt and pepper or paprika. Allow 2 eggs per serving.

SHIRRED EGGS

Use glass or glazed custard cups. Grease inside of each cup with melted butter and sprinkle liberally with matzo meal to coat well. Break fresh eggs in a saucer, one at a time, and slip into the prepared baking cups. Each cup holds one large egg or two medium-size ones. Sprinkle with salt and pepper and top with buttered matzo meal (or use matzo meal seasoned with salt, pepper, paprika or salad herbs) and place a bit of butter on top. Bake at 275° until set but not hard, approximately 10 minutes. Serve hot in the baking cups.

PASSOVER CARNATZLACH (Tiny Sausages)

1 pound ground beef	¼ teaspoon powdered garlic
1 medium-size onion, grated	a dash of red pepper
2 tablespoons water	fine matzo meal, as required
1 egg	schmaltz for frying

Combine ground beef, grated onion, water, egg, powdered garlic and red pepper to make a compact mixture. Form into little sausages not more than an inch thick and 2½ inches in length. Roll each in matzo meal or matzo cake meal. When all are formed and rolled, fry in hot melted shortening, preferably schmaltz, till nicely browned. (If possible, grill over a bed of hot charcoal.) Drain fried sausages on paper towels and slip under broiler flame before serving hot and spicy. The charcoal broiled ones are served hot from the grill.

Serves 4.

MEAT-FILLED LATKES

3 eggs	1 tablespoon grated onion
1 teaspoon salt	1 tablespoon minced parsley
1 cup cold water	hot melted shortening for deep
1¼ cups matzo meal	frying

Beat eggs with salt till creamy. Stir in, alternately, cold water and matzo meal to form a thick batter. Add grated onion and minced parsley. Refrigerate for 1 hour. Prepare filling:

Filling

1 cup chopped cooked meat	1 onion, diced
1 egg	2 tablespoons schmaltz

Combine chopped cooked meat, of any kind, with egg and onion which has been fried in schmaltz. Season to taste.

Form pancakes when batter is chilled and thick enough to handle in greased palm of left hand. Make a depression in the center of each and drop in it a ball of the prepared filling. Bring the pancake batter around and form into ovals or round flat cakes. Fry till lightly browned in deep hot melted shortening to come to the top of cakes. Turn when browned on under side and fry till nicely browned all around. Lift out and drain on paper towels. Serve with meat gravy or a fruit sauce.
Serves 4 to 6.

MULTI-LAYER PANCAKES

6 eggs, separated	2 tablespoons sugar
½ teaspoon salt	a dash of cinnamon or grated
6 tablespoons milk or water	lemon rind
6 tablespoons matzo meal	melted butter for frying
	6 ounces preserves of any kind

Beat yolks till creamy in one bowl. Beat egg whites and salt in another bowl. Stir milk or water into beaten yolks, then add matzo meal, sugar and flavoring. Stir lightly till well combined and free of lumps. Fold in beaten egg whites. Grease a heavy frying pan with melted butter and turn in about one-fourth of the batter, tilting pan to distribute evenly. Cook over moderate heat till set. Turn out on a lightly sugared serving plate. Grease pan and cook the second pancake. Spread some of the preserves on first pancake, then turn out baked second pancake evenly over the first one, repeating process till all four pancakes are stacked. Top with bits of remaining preserves and cut into 4 wedges. Serve with sour cream and/or cottage cheese for breakfast or luncheon.
Serves 4.

PASSOVER "BLINTZES"

Reduce matzo meal to half in the list of ingredients in above recipe. The batter should be thin enough to pour like heavy cream, thin enough to spread quickly when the pan is tilted. Cook over moderate heat and turn out pancake on a doubled kitchen towel. While the second pancake is cooking, spread the previous one with a mixture of cottage cheese and sour cream, flavored with grated lemon or orange rind and sugar to taste. Roll up, tucking in both ends. When all are fried and rolled, brown lightly under broiler flame and serve with additional sour cream and/or cottage cheese mixture. Or top with stewed fresh or dried fruits, preserves of any kind used for Passover, or serve plain.

PASSOVER BANANA PUDDING

2 large ripe bananas	½ cup matzo meal
2 large tart apples	¼ teaspoon cinnamon
2 tablespoons lemon juice	¼ teaspoon nutmeg
½ cup sugar	3 eggs, separated

Peel and slice bananas. Sprinkle lightly with powdered sugar and let stand at room temperature while preparing the pudding. Grate unpared apples into a mixing bowl. Add lemon juice, sugar, matzo meal and spices, then fold in beaten egg yolks till well combined. Turn into a well-greased pudding dish or shallow casserole and bake at 325° till set, about 25 minutes. The edges of pudding should be lightly browned. Turn out on a serving plate or platter. Cover with prepared sliced bananas and top with stiffly beaten egg whites. Slip under the broiler flame to brown lightly just before serving time. Good hot or cold, with either fish or meat meals, as a special dessert.

Serves 6.

CARROT PUDDING

2 cups grated raw carrot, tightly packed	½ cup potato flour
	1 cup shredded apple
2 tablespoons matzo meal	½ cup good wine
1 cup, sugar	grated rind of 1 lemon
8 eggs, well beaten	2 tablespoons lemon juice

Combine ingredients in the order listed and turn into a well-greased pudding dish. For shortening use either peanut oil or rendered goose fat for best results. Bake 45 minutes at 375° or till lightly browned. Serve hot with or without sauces such as applesauce, cranberry sauce or stewed rhubarb. Good served cold, too.

Serves 6.

MATZO FARFEL PUDDING

2 cups matzo farfel
1 quart boiling water
4 eggs, separated
½ cup sugar
1 teaspoon salt

4 tablespoons hot fat (schmaltz or oil)
1½ cups diced dried fruits (prunes, pears, etc.)
¼ cup chopped walnuts

Pour boiling water slowly over farfel, then drain well. Beat egg yolks with sugar till smooth. Stir in prepared farfel, adding salt and beaten egg whites. Heat shortening to be used in a pudding dish or casserole and add to first mixture, stirring well. Add the dried fruit and chopped nuts. Turn mixture into greased pudding dish and bake 45 minutes at 350° or till nicely browned on top. Serve from casserole or turn out on a heated platter. Garnish with more chopped nuts and serve hot with Lemon or Orange Sauce. (See pages 104, 105, 106.)
Serves 6.

FRUITED VEGETABLE KUGEL

½ cup matzo meal
¾ cup sugar
½ teaspoon cinnamon or nutmeg
½ teaspoon salt
1 teaspoon grated lemon rind
2 tablespoons lemon juice

1 cup each grated carrot, tart raw apple, white potato and sweet potato
¼ cup raisins
½ cup dates, figs and/or prunes chopped or diced fine
½ cup hot melted schmaltz

Combine all dry ingredients in a mixing bowl, then add the grated lemon rind and juice. Prepare the remaining ingredients and pack tightly for measuring each in turn. Heat the schmaltz in the pudding dish to be used and combine both mixtures before stirring in the hot fat. Turn into the greased pudding dish and bake 50 to 60 minutes at 350° or till nicely browned. Serve plain or with Lemon Sauce. Or top each portion with stewed fresh or frozen rhubarb, slightly sweetened.
Serves 6 to 8.

MATZO SHALET

4 matzos
6 eggs, separated
½ cup sugar
¼ teaspoon salt
¼ teaspoon cinnamon

1½ cups grated tart apple
¼ cup seedless raisins
¼ cup chopped walnuts or almonds and pecans
1 teaspoon grated lemon rind
2 tablespoons lemon juice

Soak matzos in water to cover while beating egg yolks in a large mixing bowl. Squeeze water from matzos and add to beaten yolks. Stir well, adding sugar, salt and cinnamon while combining. Combine grated apple, raisins, nuts, lemon rind and juice in another bowl. Let stand while beating egg whites stiff but not dry. Combine the first two mixtures, then fold in beaten egg whites. Turn into a well-greased casserole or pudding dish and bake 45 to 55 minutes at 350° or till nicely browned on top. Serve hot from the pudding dish or casserole, either plain or with stewed dried fruits, slightly sweetened.

Serves 6.

CHEESE AND MATZO PUDDING (Basic Recipe)

4 matzos	2 cups milk
lukewarm water to cover	grated rind and juice of 1 lemon
1 pound dry cottage cheese	¾ cup sugar
4 eggs	1 teaspoon salt
	4 tablespoons melted butter

Soak matzos in a large container with enough lukewarm water to cover. Let stand only while preparing the other ingredients. Drain or press out water carefully to avoid breaking matzos. Put cheese through a coarse strainer. Beat eggs with a rotary beater and stir in milk, grated lemon rind, lemon juice, sugar and salt. Melt butter in a square pan, 8 x 8 inches, not more than 2 inches deep. Turn the pan so that sides as well as bottom will be amply greased. Turn excess melted butter into the liquid mixture. Place one drained matzo in bottom of pan, spread with one third of the sieved cheese. Top with second matzo, spread with second portion of cheese and do the same with the third matzo. Top with remaining matzo and turn egg and milk mixture over slowly. Bake 1 hour at 375° or till nicely browned on top and firm to the touch. Serve hot or cold, with or without stewed fruit or berries.

Serves 8.

Passover Pudding Sauces

LEMON SAUCE

1 cup sugar	2 eggs, separated
1 cup cold water	1 tablespoon potato flour
¼ cup lemon juice	a dash of salt
a little grated lemon rind	

Combine sugar, water, lemon juice and grated rind in top of a double boiler over hot water, or cook over low heat in a saucepan, stirring till the mixture begins to boil. Beat egg yolks and stir in. Moisten the potato flour and salt with a little cold water and stir in till smooth. Cook, stirring constantly till the sauce is clear and thickened. Beat egg whites and fold in. Can be used hot or reheated over boiling water.

ORANGE SAUCE

Add 4 tablespoons of orange juice to the lemon juice in the above recipe. Omit grated lemon rind. Increase to 3 eggs and proceed in the order given for Lemon Sauce. Grated orange rind may be added last if desired, a few bits at a time, for added color.

WINE SAUCE

½ cup honey	2 eggs, separated
½ cup cold water	1 cup red wine
1 tablespoon potato flour	1 teaspoon grated lemon or orange
a pinch of salt	rind (optional)

Combine honey, water and potato flour in a saucepan and cook over low heat, stirring constantly till thickened and smooth. Add salt and beaten egg yolks, stirring in till smooth. Remove from heat. Beat egg whites and fold in. Stir in wine and grated rind just before serving time.

RAISIN SAUCE (Basic Recipe)

½ cup chopped seeded raisins	2 tablespoons butter or vegetable
1½ cups water or canned fruit	shortening
juice	1 tablespoon potato flour
¼ cup sugar	1 tablespoon cold water
a dash of salt	

Cook chopped raisins, liquid, sugar and salt together over low heat 5 to 10 minutes, stirring to prevent lumping. Add shortening. Stir potato flour with tablespoon of cold water and stir in, cooking one to two minutes longer or till sauce is clear. Serve hot or cold.

Yields approximately 2 cups sauce.

YEAR-ROUND PUDDING AND DESSERT SAUCES
Stewed Rhubarb and Strawberries

1½ cups stewed fresh, canned or	1 cup sliced fresh or frozen
frozen rhubarb	strawberries, cut or whole
	sugar or honey to taste

Combine and cook 3 minutes over moderate heat.

Yields 2 cups sauce.

Stewed Red Raspberries and Applesauce

1½ cup fresh, canned or frozen
    berries

1½ cups applesauce, sweetened to
    taste
3 drops red vegetable coloring

Combine and cook 5 minutes over moderate heat the fresh or frozen berries. Add applesauce and sweeten to taste with sugar or honey. Add coloring and stir well before using. Canned berries need heating only.
Yields 2½ cups sauce.

Thickened Orange and Pineapple Sauce

2 tablespoons cornstarch or po-
    tato flour
¼ cup sugar

1 cup fresh or canned orange
    juice
1 tablespoon lemon juice
1½ cups canned crushed pineapple,
    juice included

Combine cornstarch and sugar then stir in fruit juices and cook over low heat, stirring till thick and clear. For Passover, use potato flour in place of cornstarch. Cool before stirring in the crushed canned pineapple and syrup till free of lumps.
Serves 6 to 8.

Lemon Sauce

2 eggs or 3 yolks
¼ cup sugar
a pinch of salt

6 tablespoons lemon juice
1 tablespoon grated lemon rind

Beat eggs with sugar till creamy. Add salt, lemon juice and grated rind. Cook over hot water or in top of double boiler, stirring till thickened.
Yields 1 cupful.

PASSOVER SALAD DRESSINGS

½ cup lemon juice
1 cup peanut oil (special for
    Passover use)
1 teaspoon salt

¼ cup sugar
½ teaspoon paprika (for Passover
    use)
1 teaspoon onion juice (optional)

Combine all ingredients in a bottle or glass jar. Cover tightly and shake well before using.
Yields 1½ cups.

Variation 1: For salads to serve with milchig meals, stir in sour cream to thicken dressing and add minced parsley.

Variation 2: For salads to serve with fish meals, add well-chopped pickled beets and/or chopped hard-cooked eggs to basic dressing or Variation 1.

Variation 3: For chicken or other meat salads, add 1 tablespoon beet-colored horseradish and 2 tablespoons minced parsley and/or celery leaves.

Variation 4: For fresh fruit salad topping, stir in enough sour cream to thicken basic dressing, then flavor with orange juice, pineapple juice or a little wine—just enough to make the dressing of desired consistency.

PASSOVER BANANA CAKE

7 eggs, separated	1 cup mashed ripe bananas
1 cup sugar	¾ cup matzo cake meal
¼ teaspoon salt	¼ cup potato flour
	½ to 1 cup coarsely chopped nuts

Beat egg yolks with sugar till light and creamy. Combine salt, mashed bananas, cake meal and potato flour. Add to beaten yolks, a little at a time, while stirring to combine into a smooth batter. Beat egg whites stiff but not dry, adding a pinch of salt for quicker action, and fold into the batter as lightly as possible. Fold in chopped nuts very lightly. Turn mixture into a lightly greased spring form cake pan and bake 40 to 45 minutes at 325° or till lightly browned on top. Cool in the cake pan on a wire rack or place the cake pan so that it rests on two inverted pans of equal size to permit the circulation of air under baked cake. When cold, remove from pan and decorate with the following frosting:

Frosting

1 egg white, beaten slightly	a pinch of salt
⅞ cup sugar	3 tablespoons cold water

Combine ingredients in the order listed in top of a double boiler and place over boiling water. Keep water at boiling point while using a rotary beater for 7 minutes or till the mixture becomes thick enough to spread easily. Let cool slightly before decorating cake. Work rapidly before the frosting hardens.

PASSOVER CHOCOLATE CAKE

1 cup sugar	7 eggs, separated
¾ cup matzo cake meal	grated rind and juice of 1 orange
3 tablespoons Passover cocoa	or lemon
¼ teaspoon salt	3 tablespoons cold water
	½ cup finely ground almonds

Sift together dry ingredients into a mixing bowl. Beat egg yolks till creamy and stir into dry mixture, adding the grated orange or lemon rind, cold water and fruit juice a little at a time till well combined. Stir in ground almonds last and fold in stiffly beaten egg whites. Turn into a lightly greased and matzo cake meal dusted spring form cake pan and bake 50 minutes at 325° or till the cake springs back when touched lightly with the forefinger. Let cool in the pan hung on the neck of a stout bottle or strong funnel so that air circulates under and around cake. Serve plain or with the following frosting:

Frosting

2 ounces chocolate from Israel	3 to 4 tablespoons melted butter
(unsweetened kind)	or all-purpose vegetable short-
1 cup powdered sugar	ening
a dash of cinnamon	

Melt chocolate in top of a double boiler over hot water. Stir in sugar and cinnamon till heated through and liquefied, then add melted butter or shortening, stirring lightly. Drizzle this over top of cake in any desired pattern. Or if cake is inverted, let this frosting flow lightly over top of cake from the saucepan while warm, running down sides of cake.

PASSOVER NUT CAKE

8 eggs, separated	1 tablespoon lemon juice
8 tablespoons sugar	2 tablespoons matzo cake meal
½ teaspoon grated lemon rind	1 cup finely ground almonds or
	pecans

Beat egg yolks light, then add sugar while continuing to beat till well blended. Stir in grated lemon rind and juice, then matzo cake meal and ground nuts till well blended. Beat egg whites and fold in. Turn into an ungreased spring form cake pan and bake 1 hour at 300° or till the cake springs back when lightly pressed with the forefinger. Remove from oven and invert over a large funnel till cold before removing from cake pan. Or hang the inverted cake on the neck of a stout wine bottle till cold. Air must circulate under and around this cake till it cools.

Caution: The almonds or pecans used must be ground to a fine meal consistency, light and fluffy. *Do not use coarsely ground or chopped nuts* in this cake.

NUT KUCHEN FOR PASSOVER

6 eggs, separated
6 tablespoons sugar
6 tablespoons matzo cake meal

1 tablespoon lemon juice
½ cup finely chopped almonds or walnuts
a pinch of salt

Cream egg yolks with sugar till light lemon-colored. Add matzo cake meal gradually, stirring after each addition until very smooth. Stir in lemon juice and chopped nuts. Beat egg whites with salt till stiff but not dry and fold in lightly. Turn mixture into an ungreased tube form cake pan or a spring form cake pan and bake 45 minutes at 300°, then increase heat to 325° and continue baking 15 minutes longer or till the cake is set and lightly browned on top. Remove from oven and invert to cool over a cake rack.

PASSOVER SPONGE CAKE (Rectangular Form)

12 eggs, separated
2 cups sugar
1 lemon, grated rind and juice

¼ cup cold water
1 cup matzo cake meal sifted with
1 cup potato flour

Beat yolks with sugar till thick and creamy. Add lemon juice, grated rind and cold water, stirring well. Stir in a little at a time the sifted cake meal and potato flour till it makes a thick batter. Beat egg whites (with a pinch of salt for quicker action) till stiff but not dry and fold into batter very lightly. Line a large rectangular cake pan with white paper and turn in the batter. Bake at 325° for 50 minutes to 1 hour. The cake is done when the edges begin to be crisp, turn up slightly and stand away from sides of pain. Another test is to insert a toothpick in center of cake, and if it comes out dry, the cake is done. Turn out on a wire rack to cool before removing paper. Or cut into squares or diamond shapes, as needed, removing only as much of the paper as necessary.

This recipe makes a large-size cake, depending on depth of baking pan.

PASSOVER GINGERBALLS (also called Ingberlach)

3 eggs
1½ cups matzo meal
4 tablespoons ground ginger

1 cup honey
1 cup sugar
½ cup chopped blanched almonds

Beat eggs in a mixing bowl and stir in matzo meal and ground ginger. Let stand while bringing the honey and sugar to a boil in a deep sauce-

pan. Reduce heat and let cook at a simmer while forming the "dough"
into one-inch balls, smaller if desired. These balls may be dropped from
the tip of a teaspoon, if more convenient, into the hot syrup. Cook 10 to
12 minutes over moderate heat, taking care that contents do not boil over.
Push down with bowl of spoon from time to time. The syrup should be
absorbed and the Gingerballs lifted out with a fork to cool on a greased
flat plate or platter. Sprinkle with chopped almonds while warm.

Yields approximately 36.

PASSOVER KOMISHBRODT

4 eggs, separated	1½ cups matzo meal
1 cup sugar	¼ cup potato flour
¼ cup finely ground almonds	½ teaspoon salt
½ cup slivered blanched almonds	1 tablespoon lemon juice

Beat egg yolks and sugar till creamy. Add ground almonds a little at a
time till well combined. Stir in slivered almonds together with matzo
meal, potato flour and salt. Beat egg whites stiff but not dry and fold in.
Add lemon juice to form a thick batter. Let stand 15 to 20 minutes or till
thick enough to form into 4 rolls. Place these rolls on a lightly greased
baking pan several inches apart. Pat them to ½-inch thickness. Brush
lightly with a little sugar and water and bake 25 to 30 minutes at 350°
or till lightly browned and glazed on top. Remove from oven and slice
into 1-inch wide diagonal cuts.

Yields approximately 30 slices.

ALMOND MACAROONS

1 pound blanched almonds, finely ground	1½ pounds powdered sugar
5 egg whites	5 tablespoons matzo cake meal
	grated rind of 1 lemon

Put almonds through finest blade of your food chopper. Beat egg
whites stiff but not dry and add powdered sugar a little at a time while
continuing beating with a rotary beater or fork. Fold in lightly cake meal
and grated lemon rind, then ground nuts. Drop from the tip of a spoon
on an aluminum foil- or paper-lined cookie sheet, leaving about an inch
each way between drops. Bake at 300° from 15 to 18 minutes or till lightly
browned on top and bottom. When cool peel off paper or aluminum foil.

Yields 36 to 40.

CHOCOLATE NUT BARS

2 ounces chocolate (imported from Israel)
½ cup all-purpose shortening
⅛ teaspoon salt
1 cup sugar beaten with 2 eggs

1 tablespoon instant coffee powder
½ cup matzo cake meal
¾ cup chopped nuts
a dash of cinnamon

Use the bittersweet chocolate for best results. Melt chocolate in a saucepan over boiling water, add shortening (Passover kind) and stir till combined. Remove from heat. Beat salt, sugar and eggs with a rotary beater and blend into chocolate mixture as soon as cool. Sift together the instant coffee and matzo cake meal, then sift lightly into the combination, stirring in chopped nuts and cinnamon last. Turn into a well-greased 9-inch square baking pan and bake 25 to 30 minutes at 325°. For a glaze, brush top with a little sugar dissolved in cold water and bake 3 to 5 minutes longer. Cut in the pan while warm into 1½ by 3 inch bars. Remove from pan when cold, using a spatula or pancake turner.

Yields 18 bars.

PASSOVER PIE CRUSTS OR PIE SHELLS

Brazil Nut Crust

1½ cups ground Brazil nuts (about ¾ pound unshelled nuts)

3 tablespoons sugar
3 tablespoons matzo cake meal

Combine and press the mixture evenly with the back of a tablespoon against bottom and sides of 9-inch pie pan. Bake 6 to 8 minutes at 400° or till lightly browned at the edges. Cool before filling.

Cake Crumbs Crust

¼ cup Passover all-purpose shortening

¼ cup sugar
1⅓ cup fine sponge cake crumbs

Cream shortening and sugar and work in finely rolled sponge cake crumbs. Press against bottom and sides of a 9-inch pie pan. Bake 5 to 6 minutes at 425° or till lightly toasted before filling.

Matzo Meal Crust

1 cup matzo meal
4 tablespoons all-purpose shortening

1 teaspoon sugar
a pinch of salt

Combine ingredients with a fork and press the mixture evenly against bottom of pie pan. With bowl of a spoon bring it up the sides of pan.

Bake 5 to 8 minutes at 400° or till the fat has melted evenly and the crust becomes light yellow or lightly browned at edges. Let cool before filling.

Matzo Pie Crust

2 matzos	2 eggs
cold water to cover	2 tablespoons sugar
1 tablespoon schmaltz	$\frac{1}{8}$ teaspoon salt
or all-purpose shortening	$\frac{1}{8}$ teaspoon grated lemon rind

Soak matzos in cold water to cover for 5 minutes, then squeeze dry. Add melted shortening, eggs, sugar, salt and grated lemon rind. Combine by mixing thoroughly with a fork. Press against bottom and sides of an 8- or 9-inch pie pan that has been greased with the same shortening used for the mixture. Make the crust as thin as possible without leaving open spaces. Bake 8 to 10 minutes at 400° or till lightly browned before filling with mixture which requires further baking. If an unbaked filling is to be used, let the baked crust cool first.

PASSOVER PIE FILLINGS

Lemon Fluff Filling

1 cup sugar	3 eggs, separated
1½ cups cold water	grated rind of 1 lemon
3 tablespoons potato flour	4 tablespoons lemon juice
	a pinch of salt

Bring sugar and cold water to a quick boil in a saucepan. Moisten the potato flour with a little of the lemon juice and stir in till smooth. Beat egg yolks creamy and stir in, stirring vigorously till well combined. Cook over low heat for 3 to 5 minutes or till the mixture is clear and free from lumps. Continued stirring while cooking is advised. Let cool. Stir in grated lemon rind and remaining lemon juice and turn mixture into baked crust.

Beat eggs whites with a pinch of salt till stiff and spread over top of filling in a swirl design. Slip under the broiler flame to brown lightly before serving.

This filling is especially good with Matzo Pie Crust, but may be used with equal success with any of the other pie crusts.

Cheese and Sour Cream Filling

9 ounces cream cheese	a dash of nutmeg
3 tablespoons sugar	1 cup sour cream
1 tablespoon honey	2 tablespoons sugar
2 eggs, separated	4 tablespoons fine cake crumbs

Cream the cheese, sugar and honey till smooth and add one egg yolk at a time while creaming till combined. Add nutmeg and fold in stiffly beaten egg whites. Turn into prepared, baked pie crust and bake 8 minutes at 375° or till lightly browned at edges and on top. Combine sour cream with sugar and spoon over top of baked pie. Sprinkle the cake crumbs around in a swirl pattern or as a border. Return to oven for 5 minutes. Remove pie and let cool away from draughts. Chill in refrigerator at least 3 hours before serving.

Lemon Filling

1½ cups water	1 tablespoon honey
4 tablespoons lemon juice	3 eggs, separated
1 tablespoon grated rind	3 tablespoons potato flour
½ cup sugar	3 tablespoons cold water
	a pinch of salt

Combine water, lemon juice and grated rind, sugar and honey in a saucepan or top of double boiler. Cook over moderate heat, stirring till it begins to boil. Beat egg yolks and combine with potato flour moistened with cold water, then stir into the hot mixture. Continue to cook 10 minutes, stirring continuously. Cool. Beat egg whites with salt till stiff and fold into the mixture when cold. Turn into prepared baked pie crust. Serve when cold.

PASSOVER PUFFS

1 cup boiling water	¼ pound butter or other shortening
⅛ teaspoon salt	1 scant cup matzo meal
1 teaspoon sugar or honey	3 eggs
	¼ teaspoon grated lemon rind

Milchig: Add salt, sugar or honey and butter to the boiling water all at once and stir briskly till it bubbles again. Add the matzo meal and stir vigorously over reduced heat for 2 to 3 minutes or till the ball of dough stands away from sides of saucepan. Remove from heat. Let cool 5 minutes, then add one egg at a time, beating well after each addition. Blend in grated rind. Line a cookie sheet with aluminum foil, or if an aluminum cookie sheet is used, grease it well. Drop the mixture from a teaspoon about 1 inch apart each way. Bake at 425° for 10 minutes, then lower heat to 400° for 20 minutes longer or till lightly browned. Let cool before filling. May be kept for a day or two before filling. Can be warmed in a moderate oven, if preferred, then filled as suggested below.

Yields 36 to 40 two-inch puffs.

Fleishig: Substitute an equal amount of schmaltz or all-purpose shortening for the butter and omit sugar or honey.

Pareve: Use olive oil or all-purpose shortening only. For fish fillings, omit sugar or honey and add a pinch of pepper. A few drops of lemon juice in the liquid add flavor but are not necessary.

FILLINGS FOR PASSOVER PUFFS

Milchig

Cottage cheese mixed with preserves and chopped nuts. Thick applesauce to which chopped nuts has been added. Dried fruits, stewed and puréed, then flavored with honey, cinnamon or powdered ginger and ground almonds to make a thick paste. Adding a little sour cream and/or cream cheese makes a wonderful filling.

Fleishig

Finely chopped cooked chicken, turkey, goose breast or lamb roast mixed with fried onion, chopped *greben,* minced parsley and 1 egg yolk per cup of meat mixture, tightly packed. Cook in a frying pan only till heated through, then use as filling for cold or reheated puffs.

Pareve

Chopped hard-cooked eggs, minced parsley or green pepper. Season with salt and pepper and moisten with a mixture of oil and lemon juice to which a little sugar has been added to cut the oil taste.

Mashed Gefilte Fish or other boiled, broiled or baked fish mixed with hard-cooked egg yolks, minced parsley and/or chopped celery. Moisten with Passover Salad Dressing. Chill before filling puffs.

Charoses

2 cups grated tart apple, tightly packed	½ cup chopped almonds, pecans or walnuts
3 tablespoons honey	½ teaspoon cinnamon
	⅛ teaspoon ground ginger
	wine to moisten

Fill puffs and serve at once.

Note: With the point of a paring knife make a slit in the side of each puff for easy filling.

PASSOVER JAM ROLLS

3 eggs, separated
½ cup matzo cake meal
¼ teaspoon salt
½ teaspoon sugar

1 cup milk or water or half and half
6 ounces Passover jam or preserves
2 tablespoons mixed sugar and cinnamon

Beat egg yolks creamy. Stir in matzo meal, salt and sugar alternately with the liquid to make a smooth batter. Beat egg whites stiff but not dry and fold in. The batter should be of pouring consistency, thick as cream. Pour in a thin stream from a pitcher on a lightly greased frying pan or griddle over moderate heat, tilting the pan to distribute the batter evenly. Cook till lightly browned on under side and dry on top. Turn out, top side down on a double fold of paper towel and spread with jam or preserves while hot. Roll up each pancake while the next one is cooking. When all pancakes are rolled up, place them on a shallow pan, sprinkle with sugar and cinnamon mixture and slip under the broiler flame for 2 to 3 minutes to brown lightly just before serving time.

Yields 6 to 8.

SWEETS IN ORANGE CUPS

Allow 1 cup cooked, mashed sweet potato for two orange halves.

Season with honey, a dash of powdered ginger or cinnamon and add 1 tablespoon matzo cake meal. Moisten with orange juice and beat well till fluffy. Pile into large orange shells (after squeezing juice for breakfast) and slip under the broiler flame for 2 to 3 minutes to brown lightly on top.

Serve around roast poultry or other roasts.

PASSOVER BEET PRESERVES

3 pounds fresh beets
1 pound honey
1 pound sugar

2 tablespoons ground ginger
½ pound blanched, slivered almonds

Cook the beets in cold water to cover until tender. Drain and slip skins as soon as cold enough to handle. Cut into dice or strips. Bring honey, sugar and ginger to a boil over moderate heat in a large enough pot or saucepan to hold the beet bits. Drop in the cut-up beets and cook over low heat until the syrup has been almost absorbed, approximately 30 minutes after the boiling stage is reached. Do not stir the mixture during the cooking process but shake the pot from time to time to prevent sticking or scorching. Stir in the slivered almonds gently and turn into jelly glasses or a stoneware crock. Store away from light in a moderately cool place to prevent discoloration.

PASSOVER BLACK RADISH PRESERVES

3 pounds medium-size black
    radishes
cold water to cover

1 pound honey
1 pound sugar
1 cup slivered, blanched almonds
3 tablespoons ground ginger

Scrub the radishes thoroughly before paring and cutting into thin strips like julienne potatoes. Cover with cold water, bring to a quick boil, then let cook over reduced heat for 10 minutes. Drain well. Cover with fresh cold water and cook 10 minutes. Drain and add honey and sugar while the strips are still hot. Shake the pot in order to distribute the sweetening but do not stir with a spoon or fork. Cook over low heat for 10 minutes or until the honey and sugar are well blended. Turn up the heat slightly every five minutes until the bubbling syrup has been absorbed and the mass is a heavy preserve consistency and a rich golden brown in color. Turn off the heat and stir in the slivered almonds and ginger, alternately, a little at a time. Use two forks. Turn the preserves into jelly glasses or a stoneware crock. Do not cover until cold. Store away from light.

HOMEMADE PASSOVER YOGURT

1 tablespoon heavy sour cream   4 ounces of milk

Combine by stirring well, and let stand at room temperature 24 hours or till firm. Chill before serving with a dash of cinnamon and sugar. *This makes one serving.*

Make as many of these as required each day and keep up this regular custom the year 'round. Custard cups of ovenware or glass make excellent containers for this yogurt special.

Variation 1: Serve over fresh or frozen fruit or berries.

Variation 2: Serve with slices of bananas sprinkled with sugar and a dash of nutmeg or cinnamon.

Variation 3: Serve with pancakes or Fried Matzo instead of sour cream or other topping.

LAG B'OMER

In the Hebrew calendar of festivals, Lag B'Omer, called "the youngest of all Jewish Festivals," is celebrated in honor and remembrance of Bar Kochba and his loyal followers in their rebellion against ancient Roman restrictions. This brave band of men took their stand against religious tyranny about sixty years after the destruction of the Second Temple. Their followers were scholars and intellectuals who maintained their right to study the Torah, to teach Jewish law, to perpetuate their identity as Jews.

This festival is celebrated on the 18th of Iyar, about three weeks after Passover, usually in the month of May of the common calendar. During the weeks between Passover and Shevuoth, the days of the *Omer* (literally meaning "sheaves" in Hebrew) were counted before celebrating the final harvest when new meal or flour would be made into loaves of bread for the traditional blessing. It probably had its origin early in the history of the Jewish people, for it is first mentioned in Leviticus 23:15—"from the first sheaf of barley offered in the sanctuary, the seven weeks should be counted before celebrating."

During this period weddings are prohibited, and no public functions are indulged in. It is a period of austerity. At the end of the subdued period, it is customary in Israel today to conduct a folk festival. In many communities exhibits of books and works of art are held during the week when Lag B'Omer occurs.

Foods traditionally associated with this festival are *b'ob*, boiled and salted, eaten like the salted peanuts of the western world. The *favah* or broad bean is also served in the same manner. It is also a popular custom to eat *nahit* (chick peas) in Israel and wherever Jews gather to celebrate Lag B'Omer.

B'OB

These large, flat, dark-colored beans can be purchased at Jewish groceries and food shops. They are dried, much like lima beans, and should be soaked overnight in cold water to cover, just as with the large limas.

Drain well. Cover with fresh water and cook over moderate heat at least 45 minutes or till tender enough to pierce with a fork or toothpick. Drain well. Spread in a shallow pan and dust generously with table salt, while warm. Serve like salted peanuts when cold.

One pound of cooked *b'ob* will serve 8 to 10.

FAVAH OR BROAD BEANS

These members of the bean family are similar to B'ob and should be prepared in the same way for serving, like salted peanuts, especially at Lag B'Omer festivals.

NAHIT (Chick Peas, also called Garbanzos and Checci)

These are pointed yellow peas which require soaking overnight and cooking in the same manner as B'ob and Favah or Broad Beans when they are to be served in the same way as salted peanuts. *Nahit* is nutty in flavor when cooked. It never cooks apart no matter how long it is boiled. The cooked *nahit* can be purchased in cans at any food shop. Drained well and dusted with salt, they are delicious out-of-hand tidbits served on many occasions, especially for Lag B'Omer celebrations. For Brith Millah Ben Zocher and Pidyon 'a Ben celebrations, these are served like salted peanuts or bonbons, in small dishes, at the sweets table.

Nahit can also be used in combination with rice, with or without meat.

SHEVUOTH, FEAST OF WEEKS

This spring festival comes on the sixth (and seventh) day of the Hebrew month Sivan, in the month of May, according to the general calendar in use today. In Israel it is celebrated only one day, while custom in other countries makes it a two-day holiday, except in Reform Liberal Temples.

This festival is twofold in character. The first day is observed with a special service based on the lesson from the Pentateuch dealing with the Ten Commandments. On the second day the Giving of the Law is commemorated along with the special observance of the ancient Festival of First Fruits, perhaps dating back to the ancient sacrifices in the Temple.

Shevuoth has become accepted as the Day of Confirmation of young men and women who have completed their training in the Religious School of the Reform Liberal Temple. In Conservative Synagogues it has become customary in this country to make Shevuoth the occasion for celebrating Graduation from Religious School. This Confirmation or Graduation is not the *Bar Mitzvah* or *Bas Mitzvah* ceremonial which is celebrated on the thirteenth birthday, or day of maturity, of girls and boys. For such celebrations and suggestions for entertainment, a special section in this book has been devoted.

Shevuoth has its food associations observed throughout the world by Jews of all branches of Judaism. It is customary to serve special cheese dishes on this holiday, especially Cheese Blintzes. Dairy dishes of various kinds make up the menu, from Blintzes to Cheesecake.

BLINTZES

These delicious cheese-filled "pancakes" may have originated countless generations ago in any one of a dozen different countries. But the custom has long been established to serve Cheese Blintzes with sour cream on Shevuoth in Jewish homes everywhere.

The name probably came from the Russian *blinchiki* or *blini*. In Israel the word for cheese is *chamitah*.

Pancake Batter

2 eggs	1 tablespoon melted butter
½ cup sifted flour	pinch of salt
¾ cup water or milk and water	butter for greasing pan

Make a thin batter of beaten eggs and flour, adding the liquid gradually while mixing or beating with a fork till smooth. Add melted butter and salt, mixing well. Pour in a thin stream of batter, starting at center of heated, greased frying pan, tilting pan to distribute evenly across the bottom. Cook over low heat when starting, then increase heat as soon as pancake is smooth and firm on top and the bottom lightly browned. Turn out on a double layer of paper or linen kitchen towel, bottom side up, and spread with filling. Roll up, tucking in sides. When all the Blintzes are done, add butter to frying pan and brown on both sides or till the Blintzes are firm. Or place rolled-up Blintzes on a buttered cookie pan and brown in a moderately hot oven, top shelf. Use the oven method for browning if a double or triple recipe is used.

Cheese Filling

1 pound dry cottage cheese, or mixed cream and farmer cheese, in desired proportions	2 tablespoons sugar
	a dash of salt
1 or 2 egg yolks	a dash of cinnamon or a few drops of vanilla flavoring

Combine with a fork to a smooth and spreadable consistency, thick enough to hold its shape when placed on pancake for rolling up. If the cheese mixture is too thick, add beaten egg whites or sour cream. If too thin, thicken by adding a tablespoonful of fine cracker or dry Challah crumbs, or a rounded spoonful of mashed potato. Blintzes may be cut in two before frying.

Yields 12 Blintzes if a 10-inch frying pan is used.

ROLLED PANCAKES (French "Blintzes")

2 eggs
¼ cup powdered sugar
⅛ teaspoon salt
½ teaspoon grated lemon rind

1 cup milk
1 cup flour, sifted
½ cup preserves or jelly
confectioners' sugar

Beat eggs lightly and add sugar, salt and grated lemon rind. Add milk and sifted flour alternately while beating with a fork to form a smooth batter. Heat a 6-inch frying pan and grease lightly with butter or vegetable shortening. Pour on just enough batter to make a thin pancake, starting at the center of pan and tilting pan to spread batter evenly. Bake over moderate heat till lightly browned on under side. Turn to brown lightly and place each pancake on a kitchen towel dusted lightly with confectioners' sugar.

While the next pancake is baking, spread pancake with preserves or beaten jelly in a thin layer and roll up. When all pancakes are baked and rolled, dust with confectioners' sugar and keep warm on a heated platter or serving plate. Best when served hot with additional preserves dotted on top. Or sprinkle a little rum or brandy on each serving and light with a match.

Yields 18.

CHEESE BAGELACH (also called Rugelach)

1 recipe stretched Shtrudel dough
(see p. 23)
1 pound dry pot cheese
2 eggs

3 tablespoons sugar (optional)
3 tablespoons dry crumbs or matzo
meal
2 tablespoons melted butter

Cut the stretched Shtrudel dough into 4-inch rounds or squares. Combine cheese, eggs, sugar and crumbs. Place a ball of the mixture near one side of piece of dough and roll up quickly. Bend to form a crescent, tucking in each end. Place on a greased cookie sheet, brush with melted butter and bake 10 minutes at 425°, then decrease heat to 350° for 15 minutes or till nicely browned. Remove from pan when cool.

Yields approximately 24.

CHEESE BALLS (Mit Neshomas—Souls)

1 pound dry pot cheese (or
  farmer cheese)
3 eggs
1 teaspoon salt
3 tablespoons sugar
¼ teaspoon cinnamon

½ cup uncooked farina (or matzo
  cake meal)
3 tablespoons dry bread crumbs
¼ cup sifted flour
5 soaked and pitted prunes, well
  drained and halved
sour cream for topping, slightly
  sweetened if desired

Put the dry cheese through a soup strainer into a mixing bowl. Beat eggs, salt and sugar until creamy and stir in cinnamon, farina, bread crumbs and flour until smooth. Combine with the cheese and form into 10 balls. Press a half prune into the center of each and tuck in by rounding out carefully. Drop into rapidly boiling, slightly salted water and cook 20 minutes. Lift out balls as they rise to the top, using a perforated spoon, and keep warm in a moderate oven until serving time. Serve with a topping of sour cream. Two generally make one serving.

Yields 10.

CASSEROLE OF POTATOES AND COTTAGE CHEESE

6 medium-size potatoes, pared
  and sliced thin
1 teaspoon salt
¼ teaspoon white pepper
1 pound dry cottage cheese

4 tablespoons cracker or bread
  crumbs
3 tablespoons butter
½ cup evaporated milk or heavy
  cream

Arrange about half the sliced potatoes in a buttered casserole. Sprinkle with salt and white pepper. Press the dry cottage cheese through a strainer and cover the potato, using about half the cheese. Add remaining potato slices, dust with salt and pepper. Cover with remaining cheese. Sprinkle with crumbs, dot with butter and add the evaporated milk or cream over top. Cover and bake 45 to 50 minutes at 350° or till potatoes are tender. Remove cover and brown top under broiler. Serve hot. Top with sour cream if desired, or garnish with parsley.

Serves 6.

CREAM CHEESE DAINTIES

3 ounces cream cheese
¼ cup softened butter
1 cup all-purpose flour
a pinch of salt

2 tablespoons cream
strawberry preserves or marmalade
1 egg yolk diluted with 1 teaspoon water
confectioners' sugar

Combine cream cheese with softened butter and work in flour and salt with a pastry blender or use fingers lightly. Add cream and work it in till smooth. This makes a ball of dough the size of a large apple. Chill in the refrigerator 2 hours at least before rolling out on a lightly floured board to ¼-inch thickness. Cut into 2-inch squares and place a little bit of the preserves or marmalade in the center of each. Pinch together two opposite corners and place on a cookie sheet. Brush the top of each with diluted egg yolk and sprinkle with confectioners' sugar. Bake 12 minutes at 425° or till lightly browned and glazed on top.

Yields 24 to 30.

CHEESECAKE, SOUR-CREAM TOPPED

⅛ pound of butter
1¼ cups fine cookie or zwieback crumbs

a dash of cinnamon or nutmeg (optional)

Combine softened butter and fine crumbs, adding the spice if desired. Use a fork for best results. Press firmly over bottom of a spring form cake pan, bringing the mixture up the sides about 1 inch. Let stand at room temperature while preparing the filling, as follows:

Filling

1½ pounds cream cheese
1 cup sugar

4 eggs
1 teaspoon vanilla

Blend cream cheese and sugar till smooth. Add one egg at a time, beating after each addition. Add the vanilla last, folding in lightly. Turn mixture into crumb-lined cake pan and bake 35 minutes at 350° or till center is firm to the touch. Let cake cool in the cake pan in the oven, leaving oven door open. Remove from oven when cool and add the following topping:

Topping

1 pint sour cream
2 tablespoons sugar

½ teaspoon vanilla or almond extract

Combine and turn over top of cheesecake in the cake pan. Turn on the oven heat to 425° and bake cake with topping 5 to 7 minutes. The sour cream topping congeals when the cake cools.

Serves 12 to 14.

CREAM CHEESE HORNS O' PLENTY

8 ounces cream cheese
½ pound softened butter or substitute
2¼ cups all-purpose flour, sifted

⅛ teaspoon salt
1 cup confectioners' sugar
raspberry or strawberry jam
½ cup chopped nuts, your favorite kind

Combine cheese and butter with a fork in a warmed bowl. Sift together the sifted flour and salt. Stir into the softened cheese and butter
mixture till it forms a smooth ball of dough. Wrap aluminum foil around
it and chill in the refrigerator several hours or overnight. When ready
to bake, cut dough into two portions. Roll out dough on a pastry cloth
that has been well dusted with the confectioners' sugar. Make each round
of rolled-out dough about ⅛ inch thick. Spread with the jam and sprinkle
generously with chopped nuts. Cut into wedges about 3½ to 4 inches
each at the outer edge and roll up each separately. Place on a greased
cookie sheet, bringing the edges together to form a horn or crescent as
you place each piece. Bake 15 minutes at 375° or till nicely browned.
Let cool on the baking sheet before lifting them to a plate for serving.
May be dusted with confectioners' sugar if desired.

Yields approximately 16.

CHEESE KNISHES

1 package granulated yeast
¼ cup lukewarm water
2 tablespoons sugar
2 eggs

¼ cup oil or melted butter
2 teaspoons salt
3½ cups sifted flour
1 cup milk and water

Dissolve yeast in lukewarm water to which sugar has been added to
stimulate yeast action. Beat eggs slightly and combine with the shortening.
Sift together salt and flour into a mixing bowl. Make a well in the center
of the dry ingredients and stir in the yeast preparation to absorb a little
of the flour, then stir in the egg and shortening mixture alternately with
the liquid, stirring till most of the dry ingredients have been absorbed
and the ball of dough can be handled with the fingers. Turn out on a
board and knead about 5 minutes or till smooth and elastic. Return ball
of dough to the mixing bowl, cover with a towel and let rise at room
temperature till double in bulk, approximately 2 hours. Prepare cheese
filling while dough is rising.

Pinch off balls of dough the size of an apple and roll or flatten to
¼-inch thickness. Place a tablespoonful of the cheese mixture to be used
in the center and bring up edges to cover. With a fluted cutter scallop

the edges of half-moons and place them on a buttered cookie sheet about
1½ inches apart each way. Let rise at room temperature till light, approximately 1 hour. Brush tops with diluted egg yolk or evaporated milk or
melted butter. Bake 25 to 30 minutes at 350° or till lightly browned.

Yields 18 to 24, depending on size.

FILLINGS FOR KNISHES
Sweetened

1½ pounds dry pot cheese, sieved
2 eggs
½ teaspoon salt
4 to 6 tablespoons sugar

¼ cup dry bread crumbs or crushed
dry cereal
1 tablespoon grated lemon rind
2 tablespoons lemon juice

Combine in the order listed and chill before using.

Variation 1: Add ¼ cup chopped seeded raisins or dates and use
grated orange rind and juice in place of lemon.

Variation 2: Substitute ¼ teaspoon cinnamon and ⅛ teaspoon nutmeg
for the fruit juice and grated rind and add 3 tablespoons sour
cream.

Unsweetened

1½ pounds dry pot cheese or
farmer cheese, sieved
2 eggs
1 teaspoon salt
a dash of white pepper

4 tablespoons melted butter
1 medium-size onion, diced fine
¼ cup dry cracker or white bread
crumbs
1 teaspoon caraway seeds
(optional)

Combine sieved cheese with eggs, salt and pepper. Brown the diced
onion in hot melted butter and stir in crumbs for 1 to 2 minutes or till
lightly browned. Combine both mixtures well and add caraway seeds if
used. Let stand till cold before using.

PEPPY CHEESE SOUFFLÉ

½ pound Cheddar-type cheese
(sharp or mild)
4 tablespoons butter or substitute
4 tablespoons flour
½ teaspoon salt
¼ teaspoon each paprika and dry
mustard

1 tablespoon grated onion
a dash of cayenne pepper
(optional)
1½ cups milk
6 eggs, separated

Grate the cheese. Melt butter, or substitute, in a heavy saucepan over
low heat and add flour, stirring till blended but not brown. Add salt,

paprika, dry mustard, grated onion and cayenne pepper, if used, and stir in the milk till the mixture begins to thicken. Add grated cheese and stir slowly till melted. Remove from heat. While the mixture is cooling, beat egg yolks with a rotary beater till thick and creamy then stir in the slightly cooled creamed mixture till well blended. Beat egg whites stiff and pour cheese mixture slowly into beaten egg whites, folding the mixture in as lightly as possible. Pour into an ungreased 2-quart casserole, draw a line 1 inch from the edge all around the casserole to make a slight dent in the mixture and bake 1 to 1¼ hours at 300° so that the soufflé rises and bakes slowly for most tender results. Serve at once, plain or with mushroom sauce in a separate dish.

Serves 4 to 6.

MUSHROOM SAUCE (Basic Recipe)

4 tablespoons schmaltz or vegetable shortening	¼ teaspoon salt
4 tablespoons flour	⅛ teaspoon paprika
2 cups broth (chicken or beef) or milk	1½ cups sliced or chopped fresh mushrooms, tightly packed

Melt shortening in a frying pan. Stir in flour till deep brown. Stir in liquid gradually and cook till thickened, approximately 5 minutes. Add seasonings and mushrooms, stirring over moderate heat for 5 minutes longer.

Canned mushrooms may be substituted for the fresh variety. Onion and/or garlic salt to taste may be added for special flavor if used with fish or poultry.

Yields 2½ cups sauce.

FRUITED CHEESE RING

1 package lemon-flavored gelatin	1 green pepper, minced (optional)
1 tall can crushed pineapple	12 large maraschino cherries, cut fine
1 pound cream cheese	
1 cup chopped blanched almonds	lettuce or other greens
1 cup whipped cream	12 strips green pepper for garnish
1 cup mayonnaise	½ cup mayonnaise mixed with
	¼ cup sour cream

Dissolve the gelatin in heated pineapple juice drained from a can of crushed pineapple. Combine the crushed pineapple and cream cheese and add the almonds, whipped cream, mayonnaise, minced green pepper and cut maraschino cherries. Stir in the gelatine mixture and turn into a rinsed 10-inch ring mold. Chill at least 3 hours in the refrigerator or overnight. Unmold before serving time on a bed of greens and garnish green pepper strips. Place a tall-stem glass in the center opening of the cheese ring and fill with the mayonnaise and the sour cream dressing.

Dressing for Cheese Ring

½ cup mayonnaise
½ cup sour cream
1 tablespoon pineapple syrup from canned fruit

1 tablespoon finely diced maraschino cherries or 2 tablespoons chopped nuts
1 tablespoon sugar

Combine well and chill before serving as topping for cheese ring. Serves 10 to 12.

CARROT AND CHEESE SALAD

½ pound cottage cheese
½ cup sour cream
¼ teaspoon salt
1 tablespoon sugar

1 cup grated raw carrot, tightly packed
¼ cup chopped nuts
1 tablespoon minced parsley or green pepper

Combine ingredients in the order listed and serve on shredded lettuce or other salad greens. Top with sour cream or mayonnaise dressing if desired. Garnish with raw carrot curls or sticks.

Serves 4.

QUICK-EASY BEET BORSCHT (Basic Recipe)

1 can small whole beets
cold water as directed below
1 medium-size onion
¼ cup lemon juice or vinegar (or citric acid to taste)

3 tablespoons dark brown sugar
sour cream for thickening
hard-cooked egg slices for garnish
minced parsley, diced cucumber (optional)

Pour liquid from can of beets into a saucepan. Grate beets and add enough cold water to make one quart. Combine with beet liquid. Grate peeled onion and add, or add the whole onion cut into to permit juice to flow, then lift out onion after cooking. Bring to a boil, skim and add lemon juice or vinegar, brown sugar and salt to taste. Cook 5 minutes over moderate heat or till onion is tender. Let cool, then chill in the refrigerator about 2 hours before serving. Thicken with sour cream, stirring in about one tablespoon per serving. Add slices of hard-cooked egg, minced parsley and/or diced cucumber. Serve with plain boiled potato, steamed rice or crackers.

Serves 4 to 6.

Variation 1: Add 1 cup diced rhubarb, fresh, canned or frozen. Use only enough sweetening and sour agent to suit the taste. Cook, chill and serve as in basic recipe.

Variation 2: Grate or shred cabbage in equal amount and combine with cooked and grated beets. Use one cup cold water for each cup of tightly packed vegetable. Cook as directed in basic recipe. For Meat Borscht, cook with one pound of flanken or brisket, allowing 45 minutes or till meat is tender. Braising the meat first in the pot used is desirable, then adding the vegetables and liquid and the sweetening and souring agent. Serve hot. Thicken with beaten whole eggs.

BEET BORSCHT CONSOMMÉ

1 pound small beets
cold water to cover
½ teaspoon salt
1 small onion
¼ cup lemon juice or sour salt
crystals to taste

¼ cup dark brown sugar, or to taste
additional water to make 1 quart liquid
1 package lemon-flavored gelatin
1 cup beet liquid, heated
a pinch of ground ginger (optional)

Scrub beets and cook in cold water to cover till tender. Drain well and save the liquid. Having slipped off skins, shred or grate beets. Or dice very fine and then mash with a fork. Add salt, onion and flavoring, adding enough water to make 1 quart or 5 cups. Bring to a boil and cook only till onion is tender. Remove onion if desired.

Dissolve the gelatin in hot beet liquid, add ginger, if used, and stir into cooled Borscht. Chill in the refrigerator till thickened. Beat with a rotary beater or fork and serve in small soup bowls. Garnish with diced hard-cooked egg, diced cucumber, minced parsley or any combination desired. Float a spoonful of sour cream on top of each serving for *milchig* or *pareve* meals. For *fleishig* menu, serve plain, with or without garnish.

Serves 8 to 10.

BORSCHT FRAPPÉ

1 tall glass strained Beet Borscht
(commercial or homemade)
2 tablespoons sour cream

1 tablespoon grated cucumber (optional)
a dash of lemon juice or thin slice of lemon
topping of whipped cream

Have the Beet Borscht chilled before mixing with sour cream till smooth. Add grated cucumber and lemon juice, or place a cut or slice of lemon on edge of glass. Top with a tablespoon of whipped cream and serve in tall glasses with straws.

Individual serving.

HOME CELEBRATIONS

Many uniquely Jewish celebrations are held in the home, ranging from informal or formal gatherings to family affairs honoring the birth of a child, a confirmation, a wedding or an anniversary. In this section there are suggestions, menus and especially appropriate recipes for such occasions.

Brith Millah Celebrations (Circumcision)

It is customary to celebrate the "initiation" or *Brith Millah* of infant male children on the eight day after birth. Hospitals in almost all large cities set aside special rooms for this ceremonial. It is followed by a reception for parents, grandparents, the Mohel (ritually trained and authorized), his nurse or assistant, the relatives or friends who serve as *Quater* and *Sondeg* at the circumcision, and such friends as are invited by the happy families of the newborn.

Lekach und Branfen (honey cake and brandy) are served as a "Happy Mazel Tov" is extended. More elaborate hospitality varies from cocktails and canapés to buffet luncheon, from Gefilte Fish to roast poultry and trimmings, salads, beverages, Shtrudel or various other cakes.

Ben Zocher

This is a festive occasion for the family and friends of a newborn male child. It is celebrated the Friday evening following the birth of the baby, usually in the home of the parents. It is customary to serve wine, whiskey, brandy and cordials with honey cake or sponge cake to guests of the family. *Nahit* (boiled chick peas), well-drained after cooking till tender, and salted like salted peanuts or salted almonds, is customary fare. Canapés and cocktails have been added to the traditional *Kibbet*, hospitality.

Pidyon-'aBen

This ceremonial dates back to ancient days, perhaps the period of Jewish sojourn in the land of Egypt. It is called The Redemption of the Firstborn Son and is observed to this day by many families. It is an occasion for rejoicing one month after the birth of a first-born male child.

The traditional brandy, wine and Lekach may be augmented to include holiday dishes from chicken soup to Kugel, from "fish to nuts," depending on family custom.

Son's Bar Mitzvah, Daughter's Bas Mitzvah
or Confirmation

According to ancient law, Jewish males become of age at thirteen and are expected to assume responsibilities of membership in the congregation. Study and training having reached a certain point, the Bar Mitzvah is celebrated publicly, before the congregation and in the presence of rabbis and teachers. The *talith* or prayer shawl is donned and the celebrant given the honor of reading from the Torah.

A special recognition of the occasion is the reception tendered family and friends, immediately following services, in Synagogue or Temple, or in the home. Because the tendency to make of this celebration what spiritual leaders have called an "excuse for more Bar than Mitzvah," it is in good taste to make the celebration simple; and where at all possible, in the home of the happy celebrants.

In this section we offer a number of suggestions for entertaining in honor of son's Bar Mitzvah, daughter's Bas Mitzvah, or the confirmation ritual of the Reform-Liberal community.

Wedding Anniversaries

Wedding anniversaries are occasions for family celebration, especially the twenty-fifth (Silver) and the fiftieth (Golden).

In addition to the customary wedding cake, suitably decorated, entertainment of relatives and friends may range from simple beverages, like fruit punch, and small cakes or cookies, to many-course dinners with wines and champagnes followed by dancing.

For the Golden Wedding Anniversary, it is customary to serve a dinner beginning with Gilderne Yoich (golden chicken soup) and Mandlen (soupnuts).

Luncheons and Receptions

Youth groups, Hadassah meetings, bridal luncheons and many other events provide opportunities for entertaining at home. Simple or elaborate settings and menus will depend on the occasion. The recipes and centerpieces in this section can form a wide variety of combinations for any specific need.

Suggested Menus for Brith Millah Celebrations

Menu 1
Honey Cake and Brandy,
Cordials and Wine
Cocktail Canapés
Kasha Cocktail Knishes
Chicken Salad
Green Olives, Maslinas, Tiny
Pickles, Celery and Carrot Curls
Salted Nahit
Cookies and Small Cakes
Hot or Cold Beverages
(Depending on Weather)

Menu 2
Sponge Cake, Brandy, Cordials
and Wines
Gefilte Fish Ball Canapés
Assorted Dips for Potato Chips
Olives, Pickles and Relishes
Shtrudel
Hot or Cold Beverages
Salted Nahit, Peanuts, Glazed Nuts,
Candy, Stuffed Dates

Menu 3
Komishbrodt, Brandy, Cocktails,
Cordials, Wines
Cold Cuts
(Chicken, Turkey, Tongue, etc.)
Potato Salad, Salad Greens,
Garnishes
Relishes, Olives, Pickles, Carrot
Curls and Celery Sticks
Sponge Cake Topped with Berries
(Fresh, Stewed, Canned or Frozen)
Hot or Cold Beverages
Candied Fruits and Nuts and/or
Stuffed Prunes, Dates, Apricots

Menu 4
Cake and Brandy,
Cordials and Wines
Tiny Puffs, Assorted Cheese
and Fish Filled
Individual Fruit Salads
Small Cakes, Cookies,
Fruit Bars, etc.
Fruit Punch
Candies, Nuts, Salted Peanuts and/
or Nahit, Plumped Dried Fruits

Suggested Menus for Bar Mitzvah, Bas Mitzvah or Confirmation Celebrations

Menu 1
Fruit Punch
Torah Scroll Sandwiches
Chopped Liver Ring
Potato Salad De Luxe
Olives, Pickles
Scripture Cake
Small Cakes, Shtrudel, Cookies,
Cordials, Schnapps, Wines

Menu 2
Reception Punch
Smoked Tongue Rolls
Pastry Spirals
Crackers, Melba Toast
Jellied Tomato Flowerpots
Open Book Cake
Glazed Upside-downies, Small
Cakes, Cordials, Wines, Liquors

Suggested Menus for Bar Mitzvah, Bas Mitzvah or
Confirmation Celebrations (Cont'd)

MENU 3

Fruit Punch
Filled Tiny Puffs
Filled Beet Salad Ring

Olives, Relishes
Torah Scroll Cake
Cookies, Small Cakes, Cordials,
Wines, Cocktails

Suggested Menus for Bridal Luncheons

MENU 1

Fruit Juice Cocktail
Creamed Chicken in Toast Cups
Green Pepper Rings
Miniature Biscuits or Melba Toast
Olives, Pickles, Radish Roses
Chocolate Cake
Hot or Iced Beverages

MENU 2

Cocktails, Cocktail Canapés
Creamed Sweetbreads on Toast
Jellied Tomato Flowerpots
Relishes, Celery Curls, Olives
Sausage Cornucopias or Smoked
Tongue Rolls
Sponge Cake
Hot or Iced Beverages

MENU 3

Broiled Grapefruit Halves
Cucumber Boats
(Milchig or Pareve Filling)
Pond Lilies Salad
Pickled Beets, Olives, Relishes
Individual Challahs, Butter
Nut Cake
Hot or Iced Beverages

MENU 4

Fruit Cup
Filled Beet Salad Ring
(Cheese or Fresh Filling)
Calla Lily Sandwiches
Clover Loaf Rolls
Pineapple Meringue Cake
Ice Cream or Fruit Sherbet
Demi-Tasse

MENU 5

Fish Ball Canapés
Chicken Salad
Pineapple and Cucumber
Aspic Salad
Individual Challahs
Bridal Wreath Coffee Ring
Ice Cream
Hot or Iced Beverages

Suggestions for Wedding Receptions at Home or in Temple

Hostess Trays

Cocktails, Fruit Punch, Wines
and Liquors
Cocktail Canapés
Calla Lily Sandwiches
Tiny Puffs, Varied Fillings
Cocktail Knishes, Varied Fillings
Kosher Sausage Rolls
Smoked Tongue Rolls
Sausage Cornucopias
Quenellen

Sweets Table

Sweet-Filled Tiny Puffs
Sweet-Filled Spirals
Glazed Upside-downies
Small Cakes, Cookies
Stuffed Dates, Figs, Prunes
Raisins and Almonds
Nuts and Candy

Dips and Spreads

Potato Chips
Crackers
Toasted Biscuits
(for dipping into or spreading with):
Assorted Dips
Chopped Herring
Canapé Spreads

Hot and Iced Beverages

Demi-Tasse
Tea with Orange Slices
Soft Drinks
Mulled Cider
Fruit Punch

Buffet Table

Chicken Salad
Chopped Liver Ring
Garnishes
Salad-Stuffed Tomatoes
Potato Salad De Luxe
Cucumber Boats
Green Pepper Rings
Mogen Dovid Salad

Centerpieces for the Table

GRAPEFRUIT HOLDERS

Slice a piece from one end of a grapefruit so it will lie flat on serving platter. Put colored toothpicks through stuffed olives, tiny pickles, pickled onions, miniature pickled peppers, black olives, pickled watermelon cubes, etc., and fasten to the grapefruit in any design desired. Place celery and raw carrot curls around the base with or without parsley sprigs or curly lettuce or chicory for color.

Stud prepared grapefruit with cubes of fresh or canned pineapple chunks, cantaloupe balls, honey dew melon balls or cubes, canned pitted cherries (Royal Anne or Bing), papaya cubes or balls and a few fresh or frozen whole strawberries for color contrasts. Use plastic or wooden toothpicks.

Form inch balls of cream cheese mixtures and roll in colored sugar and ground almonds, making some green, others red and some chocolate covered. Or roll cheese balls in grated Cheddar-type cheese to which paprika has been added for color. Spear these through with colored toothpicks and stud a large grapefruit prepared to hold its place on a plate or platter. Surround with crackers, tiny biscuits, Pastry Spirals or cheese-filled Tiny Puffs.

PINEAPPLE CENTERPIECES

Select a large ripe pineapple. Cut into quarters through spears to stem end. If very large, cut into eighths. Cut off hard center fibrous core. Slip the point of a sharp paring knife between outer skin and pineapple meat. Do not remove from outer skin but cut through into half-inch pieces and stick a toothpick into each piece from the top. Now arrange the quarter or eighth sections with the spear ends outward so that the stem ends meet in the center of a large round plate or serving platter. Garnish further with green seedless grapes, large Tokay or black grapes in small clusters around the plate, and a larger bunch of grapes in the center of the centerpiece.

FRUIT PUNCH (Basic Recipe)

4 large cans pineapple juice
(1 quart-14-ounce size)
6 quarts orange juice, fresh or
frozen and diluted
4 large cans tangerine juice
(48-ounce size)
4 large cans grapefruit juice
(1 quart-14-ounce size)

1 pint maraschino cherries, red
and/or green
6 large lemons, sliced thin
6 oranges, sliced thin
fresh mint leaves
ice cubes or crushed ice
sparkling water or club soda
to taste
sugar to taste

At least one hour before serving time combine all ingredients except ice cubes, sparkling water and sugar, to be added just before use. Stir well and ladle into punch cups or paper cups from a large punch bowl. Serves 150 to 175.

Variation 1: Stud orange and lime slices with one or two cloves and let these float on top of punch.

Variation 2: Gingerale may be substituted for soda or ice water. Add just before serving time, as required.

RECEPTION PUNCH (Basic Recipe)

2 cans each grapefruit juice,
orange juice, pineapple juice,
tangerine nectar (use 48-ounce
cans)
12 lemons or limes
1½ cups canned crushed pineapple

4 cups sugar
6 quarts water
1 cup maraschino cherries, red or
green
ice cubes
mint leaves (optional)

Combine canned fruit juices and add the juice of lemons or limes, leaving two for slicing and floating on top of punch, if desired. Stir in canned crushed pineapple, sugar, water and maraschino cherries. Add the ice cubes and float fresh mint leaves on top. Let stand 10 to 15 minutes before serving from punchbowl.

Serves from 50 to 75.

Variation 1: Substitute cider for half the amount of water.

Variation 2: Add gingerale just before serving time.

Variation 3: Stir in 1 quart good brandy or cordial, for a "spiked" punch, in any of the above variations.

INDIVIDUAL CHALLAHS

1 cake or package granular yeast	3 tablespoons sugar
½ cup lukewarm water	½ cup canned or fresh orange
5 cups all-purpose flour	juice
1 tablespoon salt	½ cup oil or vegetable shortening
2 eggs	poppy seeds

Dissolve yeast in lukewarm water. Sift flour and salt together into a large bowl. Make a well in the center and stir in the yeast mixture. Beat eggs and sugar till creamy and add the orange juice and shortening or oil, stirring to combine well. Stir into the center of the yeast sponge, gradually working in the flour to form a compact ball of dough. Turn out on a board and knead till smooth and satiny. Brush the top with shortening, cover with waxpaper and chill in the refrigerator overnight.

When ready to bake, divide the dough into 24 parts to make that many 5-inch twists or Challahs. For smaller Challahs, divide the dough accordingly. Cut each portion into 3, roll between the palms into 4-inch lengths and braid together, pinching both ends securely. Place on a lightly greased cookie sheet to rise till double in bulk. Brush the top of each with diluted egg yolk and sprinkle with poppy seeds. Bake in a preheated oven at 375° for 30 minutes or till nicely browned and crusted.

Yields 24 individual Challahs of the 5-inch size or 36 smaller ones.

MOGEN DOVID BAGELS

Slice bagels in half with a sharp knife, allowing 4 halves per serving. Spread cut sides with butter, cream cheese or a combination of both. Arrange strips of lox (smoked salmon) into crossed triangles, resembling *Mogen Dovids*. May be slipped under the broiler flame for 2 to 3 minutes before serving or heated on top shelf of oven at 350° for 5 minutes. A cookie sheet will hold many of these *Mogen Dovid* Bagels and can be handled easily. Strips of pickled herring may be substituted for the lox, without broiling.

Or cut bagels and butter each cut side generously. Place strips of Cheddar-type cheese on each to form *Mogen Dovids* and slip under the broiler flame for 2 to 3 minutes to melt the cheese slightly. Serve hot, with or without paprika sprinkled over cheese.

COCKTAIL CANAPÉS

Pie Pastry Canapes

Roll pie pastry into a rectangle as thin as possible without breaking. Cut into three equal parts. Mix grated Cheddar-type cheese with caraway seeds, paprika, white pepper or garlic salt to taste. Cover one section of rolled-out pastry with this mixture and roll up from the long side as tightly as possible. Place on a buttered cookie sheet, cut side down.

Grated Cheddar cheese, combined with a little mayonnaise and prepared mustard, makes a good spread for the second section of pastry dough. Dust lightly with fine cracker or dry bread crumbs and roll up tightly. Place next to the first roll.

Combine mashed smoked sardines, hard-cooked egg yolks and enough dry crumbs to make a spreadable mixture. Season with a little lemon juice if desired. Spread on the third section of rolled-out pastry, roll up and place with the other rolls. Brush lightly with evaporated milk and bake 12 to 15 minutes at 400° or till lightly browned.

When cold, cut into ½-inch pieces, straight or diagonally. Use a sharp knife for quick and easy cutting. These may be served plain or toasted under the broiler flame for 1 to 2 minutes just before serving time.

Milchig Canapé Spreads

Cream cheese mixed with chopped nuts and sweetened to taste with confectioners' sugar or honey. Spread on crackers and top with chopped nuts or a slice of red or green maraschino cherry.

Cream cheese softened with a little sour cream and seasoned with savor-salt or powdered garlic. Spread and top with a thin slice of pimiento-stuffed green olive.

Cream cheese and mashed smoked sardines in equal portions. Add minced olives or parsley and top with a bit of canned pimiento for color.

Cream cheese and red caviar in equal portions. Top with bits of parsley or a sliver of green pepper for color contrast.

Fleishig Canapé Spreads

Chopped liver topped with minced parsley or a slice of pimiento-stuffed green olive.

Chopped cooked chicken, chopped almonds or walnuts and mayonnaise to combine. Spread and top with a bit of mixed chopped pickle relish.

Chopped tongue or corned beef moistened with mayonnaise. Spread on crackers or rounds of bread and top with thin slice of hard-cooked egg white. Place a bit of green or red pepper in center for color.

Pareve Canapé Spreads

Sliced Gefilte Fish on rounds of rye bread, topped with a sprig of parsley or a dot of beet-colored horseradish. Canned gefilte fish, either in

rolls or small balls, may be used to advantage. Slice the rolls of fish to
¼-inch thickness. Cut the cocktail-size balls of fish in halves and place
cut side down on rounds of bread, making heartier portions.

Mashed gefilte fish, seasoned with horseradish and minced parsley,
makes a good spread for crackers or bread rounds. Use bits of green or
red pepper for garnish.

Fresh carp icre (roe) may be spread on crackers or dark bread rounds
or square cuts. Top with a thin slice of pimiento-stuffed green olive, a bit
of parsley or green pepper.

Hard-cooked eggs, mashed and combined with mashed tuna fish, pink
salmon or sardines and mixed with a little mayonnaise, make good
spreads. Garnish with bit of pimiento or green pepper.

GEFILTE FISH BALL CANAPÉS

For quick-easy preparation, use the small gefilte fish balls or elongated
rolls available in glass containers at all food stores. Slice into halves the
small balls of fish and place cut side down on toasted or plain thinly
sliced rye bread which has been cut into 1½- or 2-inch rounds not more
than ⅛-inch thick. Rolls of fish may be sliced thinner. Use a cookie cutter
or thin glass for cutting bread slices. Top each canapé with a bit of
pimiento, green pepper or parsley for color contrast. Or dot with a bit of
beet-colored horseradish. Or stick a small sliver of pickle on top.

If these canapés are prepared much in advance of serving time, place
them on a tray, cover with waxpaper or aluminum foil tucked well under
the tray and store in the refrigerator or freezer.

KOSHER SAUSAGE ROLLS

Use thinly sliced bologna or salami. Remove skin casing before slicing,
diagonally if by hand, or, preferably, with a slicing machine. Wrap each
slice around a thin sliver of pickle and hold in place with colored toothpicks. Or use halves of pimiento-stuffed green olives, as in Smoked
Tongue Rolls.

SMOKED TONGUE ROLLS

Have cooked smoked tongue sliced thin at the delicatessen or food
store. Roll each slice around a thin strip of dill or sweet-sour pickle and
fasten each with a colored plastic toothpick.

Potted beef tongue, trimmed and sliced thin after chilling, may be
used in the same manner.

Allow 3 to 4 per serving.

Variations may be made by rolling the tongue slices tight and fastening with a pimiento-stuffed green olive half on each side, speared through with toothpicks. Or wrap a strip of pickled red pepper, the sweet-sour kind, and fasten with toothpick to hold pepper and rolled tongue in place.

SAUSAGE CORNUCOPIAS

These can be made by shaping each slice of salami into a cornucopia and piercing through the middle with a plastic toothpick. Fill with any of the fillings suggested below, chill one hour and serve. Or place a large stuffed green olive inside the cornucopia, holding it in place with the toothpick.

Allow 3 to 4 per serving.

Fillings

Hard-cooked eggs, chopped fine and combined with minced sausage and mayonnaise dressing. Season to taste with salt, pepper and paprika.

Combine 2 parts chopped beef liver with 1 part peanut butter. Garnish with parsley bits, or red and green pepper chopped fine.

Finely chopped tongue with hard-cooked eggs and minced pimiento olives moistened with a little mayonnaise. Use a thin strip of dill or sweet pickle for garnish.

QUENELLEN

1 pound ground beef	2 tablespoons cracker crumbs
1 onion, grated	salt and pepper to taste
1 small carrot, grated	½ cup cracker crumbs for
2 eggs	breading
	½ cup melted shortening or oil

Combine all ingredients except the ½ cup crumbs and melted shortening. Form into small balls 1 inch in diameter and roll in crumbs. Fry in hot melted shortening or oil till nicely browned. Drain on paper towels. Serve hot, speared with toothpicks for handling.

Serves 8 to 12 as hors d'oeuvres.

ASSORTED DIPS FOR POTATO CHIPS

Mayonnaise to which minced parsley and/or pickle relish has been added in any desired proportions. Serve in small glass bowls placed close to containers of potato chips.

Cream cheese and mayonnaise in equal portions, garnished with minced black or green olives, pimiento, and/or parsley.

Mashed smoked sardines, cream cheese and sour cream in any desired proportions make a welcome dip. Add a little grated lemon rind and enough lemon juice to bring out the fish flavor. Consistency should be thick enough to prevent running.

Hard-cooked egg yolks mashed to a paste with French dressing or mayonnaise and pointed up with a dash of cayenne or curry powder are delicious. Minced parsley or green pepper bits add color contrast.

COCKTAIL KNISHES

4 cups all-purpose flour	8 tablespoons ice water or fruit
1½ teaspoons salt	juice (orange or pineapple)
1¼ cups all-purpose shortening or oil	

Sift together flour and salt in a mixing bowl. Cut in shortening with a wire pastry blender or stir in oil till the mixture forms into little peas. Add liquid a little at a time while mixing with a fork to form a ball of pastry. Chill 1 hour or more in the refrigerator before rolling out to ⅛-inch thickness. Cut into 2½-inch rounds and fill with any of the following fillings. Brush with diluted egg yolk or evaporated milk, depending on type of filling. Mark the edges with a fluted cutter or the tines of a fork and bake 15 minutes at 425° or till lightly browned. Serve hot, or reheat 5 minutes at 350°.

Fillings: Cottage cheese, chopped nuts, sugar and cinnamon to taste with 1 tablespoon fine cracker or bread crumbs per cup. If cheese is too dry, add a little sour cream and/or orange juice. The mixture should be thick enough to hold its shape when placed in center of pastry rounds. Variations are made by adding chopped raisins or currants, chopped mixed candied fruits, and/or grated orange or lemon rind. Cooked kasha is combined with fried onion, and/or chopped dried fruits and chopped nuts, sweetened to taste.

Yields approximately 80.

PASTRY SPIRALS, CHICKEN-FILLED

Roll out your favorite pie pastry into a rectangle of ⅛-inch thickness. Spread with ground-up cooked chicken, *greben,* and enough mashed hard-cooked egg yolks to make a smooth spread. Season to taste. With a wide-blade knife or spatula, spread the pastry with the filling mixture and roll up, starting with the long end. Chill at least 1 hour in the refrigerator.

When ready to bake, cut the rolled-up pastry into 1-inch pieces, straight or diagonally. Place cut side down on a lightly greased cookie sheet and bake at 425° 12 to 15 minutes or till lightly browned. Remove with a spatula or pancake turner to serving platters or trays. These can be served hot or cold (but freshly baked), and eaten out of hand.

Allow 2 to 4 per serving.

Sweet-filled Spirals are made by spreading rolled-out pie pastry with a mixture of equal parts red raspberry or strawberry preserves and fine dry white bread or cracker crumbs. Adding finely ground nuts in small amounts adds special flavor. Chill thoroughly before cutting and baking. Can be baked in rolls brushed with diluted egg yolk or evaporated milk, then cut into 1-inch pieces and slipped under the broiler flame to brown lightly before serving.

PASTRY WRAP-AROUNDS

Roll out pie crust pastry to ¼-inch thickness, and cut into 1-inch strips. Wrap the pastry strips around cocktail wieners or frankfurters. Be sure to wrap the pastry diagonally. Turn in or pinch the ends together. Cocktail wieners need not be cut. The wrapped franks should be cut into 3 or 4 parts for easy handling. Chill these in the refrigerator until a half hour before serving time. Arrange cut side down on a lightly greased cookie sheet and bake at 400° 12 to 15 minutes or till nicely browned. For convenient handling, insert a toothpick in each when arranging on a service tray or platter.

Allow 4 per serving.

TINY PUFFS

2 cups boiling water	1 tablespoon sugar (optional)
1 cup butter or vegetable short-ening	1 teaspoon vanilla if using sweet or cheese filling
½ teaspoon salt	2 cups flour
	6 eggs

Add butter or other shortening to boiling water in saucepan or top of double boiler, and stir till mixed. Add salt and sugar, and vanilla if the fillings are to be sweet and/or cheese mixtures, then dump in the sifted flour all in a heap. Stir vigorously, while keeping over moderate heat, till the batter is smooth and forms a ball of dough which stands away from side of pan. Remove from heat and let cool about 2 minutes. Add one egg at a time, beating well after each addition.

Drop from a teaspoon, dipped in water or lightly greased, onto a greased cookie sheet. Allow about 1 inch each way between drops. Bake 10 minutes at 450°, then turn down heat to 400° for 20 minutes or until the puffs have risen and are very light. Remove from pan when cool and fill. Cut a slit in the side of each puff with the point of a paring knife and insert any of the following fillings, as close to serving time as possible.

Yields 72 to 80 (1½ to 2 inches in diameter).

Note: These puffs may be reheated in a 375° oven before filling. Place a small pan of hot water on bottom of oven till the puffs are heated through, about 5 minutes.

FILLINGS FOR TINY PUFFS

Sweet Milchig

1½ cups dry pot cheese, sieved
½ pound cream cheese
½ cup sour cream or whipped cream

½ teaspoon salt
6 ounces red raspberry preserves
1 teaspoon grated lemon or orange rind

Combine all ingredients in the order listed. Chill 1 hour before using as filling, allowing 1 teaspoonful per Tiny Puff.

Nippy Milchig

1½ cups dry pot cheese, sieved
1¼ cups grated or shredded Cheddar-type cheese (tightly packed)
1 tablespoon ketchup or chili sauce

1 teaspoon savor-salt
3 tablespoons mayonnaise
2 tablespoons sour cream
a dash of red pepper (optional)

Combine in the order listed. Chill 1 hour, if time permits, before filling puffs.

Pineapple and Cheese

1 pound cream cheese
4 tablespoons sour cream
½ teaspoon grated lemon or orange rind

1½ cups canned crushed pineapple, drained well, tightly packed for measuring
2 egg whites
¼ teaspoon salt

Mash cream cheese with a fork and work in sour cream, grated fruit rind and well-drained crushed pineapple. Chill 10 minutes. Beat egg whites with salt, at room temperature, and fold in lightly with a fork about 10 minutes before using.

Vanilla Cream Filling

Use one package vanilla pudding mix and follow directions on the package. Let cool before using as filling for 18 to 24 puffs.

Ice Cream Filling

Use your favorite flavor ice cream, homemade or commercial. Allow 1 tablespoonful per filling. Must be filled and served at once.

Fleishig Fillings

Chopped chicken or beef liver, combined with peanut butter and fried onion. Season with garlic salt. Add minced parsley.

Chopped liver and hard-cooked eggs, seasoned to taste and moistened with chicken or goose schmaltz.

Chopped chicken and/or *greben,* combined with minced parsley and/or mashed hard-cooked egg yolks. Season to taste.

Chopped smoked or potted tongue, combined with chopped hard-cooked eggs, pickle relish and mayonnaise.

Chopped corned beef or peppered meat, combined with chopped hard-cooked eggs, minced parsley and/or celery leaves. Moisten with mayonnaise or French dressing.

Note: One cupful of prepared mixtures is sufficient for filling 4 to 6 Tiny Puffs made with vegetable shortening or schmaltz.

Pareve Fillings

Salmon or tuna fish, combined with chopped hard-cooked eggs, minced celery and/or parsley, and moistened with enough mayonnaise to make a soft but compact filling. A few drops of lemon juice add piquancy.

Gefilte Fish, mashed with a fork and seasoned with horseradish, minced parsley and/or celery leaves, makes a good filling. Moisten with fish liquid and French dressing or mayonnaise, if desired.

Chopped herring, combined with grated raw apple and hard-cooked eggs, mashed well and moistened with lemon juice and enough brown sugar to taste. Minced parsley and/or chopped green pepper may be added if desired. Chopped pickle relish may be added.

PASTRY DOUGH FOR KNISHES

2½ cups sifted flour	¾ cup vegetable shortening
¾ teaspoon salt	5 to 6 tablespoons ice water
	a pinch of sugar (optional)

Sift together flour and salt. Cut in shortening with a wire pastry blender or two knives till the mixture resembles little peas. Add ice water a little at a time while mixing to form a ball of pastry dough. Turn out on a lightly floured board or cloth and roll out deftly and quickly to ⅛-inch thick rectangle or round. If too large a ball of pastry to handle at one time, divide into two parts, then roll each in turn as required for filling and baking. Chill pastry in refrigerator 1 hour.

Cut with a 2½-inch cookie cutter, or use a thin water glass. Pastry may be cut into squares, using a fluted cutter for scalloped-edge Knishes.

Sufficient for 36 to 48 rounds of pastry for Knishes 2½ to 3 inches in diameter.

Note: Baked Knishes may be refrigerated when cold or placed in the freezer compartment for later use. Heat before serving by placing Knishes on a cookie sheet or in other baking pan, close together and covered with aluminum foil; 5 to 10 minutes at 350° is sufficient to freshen Knishes.

Cheese Filling for Pastry Dough Knishes

1 pound dry pot cheese, sieved	½ teaspoon salt
¼ cup fine cracker crumbs	¼ cup sugar
2 eggs	1 teaspoon grated lemon rind
	2 tablespoons lemon juice

Combine with a fork to make a compact mixture soft enough to drop from a teaspoon without spreading. Place a rounded teaspoonful in center of each rolled round or square cut of pastry dough. Fold over and pinch edges together securely. Place on a lightly greased cookie sheet, brush tops with diluted egg yolk or evaporated milk for a glaze. Bake at 400° 12 minutes or till lightly browned.

POTATO DOUGH KNISHES

2 cups cooled mashed potatoes	1 teaspoon salt
2 cups sifted all-purpose flour	2 tablespoons melted shortening
3 eggs, beaten	of your favorite kind

Combine in the order listed to make a dough that is compact enough to roll out on a lightly floured board. Cut into 2½- to 3-inch rounds and flatten to desired thickness. Arrange on a lightly greased cookie sheet or shallow baking pan at least an inch apart each way. Place a heaping tablespoonful of filling in the center of each round of dough and pinch edges together into half moons, crescents or with the center seam in the middle from tip to tip. Brush tops with diluted egg yolk, melted shortening or stiffly beaten egg white. Bake 30 minutes at 350° or till nicely browned. May be baked and reheated before serving time.

Kasha Filling

1 cup buckwheat groats (medium ground)

1 egg beaten with 1 teaspoon salt

3 tablespoons melted shortening (butter, margarine, schmaltz, etc.)

2 tablespoons chopped nuts (walnuts, almonds, hazel nuts, etc.)

3 cups boiling water

sugar and cinnamon to taste (3 tablespoons sugar and a dash of spice)

2 tablespoons fine cracker crumbs

grated rind of orange or lemon (optional)

Combine groats with beaten egg and salt till grains are coated. Add to melted shortening in a heavy frying pan over moderate heat, stirring till lightly browned. Add nuts and boiling water, cover and cook over moderate heat 15 minutes or till all moisture has been absorbed. Let cool and add sugar, cinnamon, cracker crumbs and grated fruit rind. Mix well before using for filling.

Variation: Omit sugar and flavorings. Substitute finely diced fried onions and/or chopped *greben* (cracklings).

KASHA FILLINGS FOR PASTRY OR POTATO DOUGH KNISHES

Milchig

1½ cups cooked kasha

¼ cup sieved pot cheese

1 onion, diced and fried in

4 tablespoons butter

1 egg

salt and white pepper to taste

Combine in the order listed.

Sweetened kasha requires the addition of

3 tablespoons sugar

a dash of cinnamon and/or nutmeg

¼ cup chopped seeded raisins

4 tablespoons finely chopped nuts

Fried onion may be omitted, if desired.

Fleishig

1½ cups cooked kasha

½ cup finely chopped cooked chicken or other meat

1 onion, diced fine and fried in

4 tablespoons schmaltz

1 raw egg (optional)

a dash of savor—salt or mixed herbs

Combine and use for filling rounds or squares.

Variations may be made by substituting chopped smoked tongue, peppered meats or corned beef bought at foodshops or delicatessen. Combine with the other ingredients listed. Chopped *greben* may be used with any of the meat combinations as a substitute for diced fried onion.

Note: See also Fleishig Fillings for Tiny Puffs.

CHOPPED LIVER RING

2 pounds chicken or beef liver, broiled and chopped
4 hard-cooked eggs
2 large onions, diced fine
½ cup schmaltz or salad oil
1 cup peanut butter
salt, garlic powder, paprika to taste

1 tablespoon schmaltz for greasing ring mold
8 to 10 large pimento-stuffed green olives, sliced
strips of green or red pepper for garnish
parsley, salad greens, radish roses, Maslinas

Put the chopped liver and hard-cooked eggs through the fine blade of your food chopper. Brown the diced onions in hot melted schmaltz or oil and blend in with a fork, along with the peanut butter and seasonings. Coat the inside of an 8-inch ring mold with the spoonful of schmaltz and arrange the slices of pimento-stuffed olives in the bottom and up the side of ring mold. Press in an inch depth of the chopped mixture to prevent the slices from slipping, then press in the remaining liver mixture. Cover with waxpaper and chill until ten minutes before serving time. Dip the bottom of the ring mold in hot water for a few seconds and unmold on a serving platter. Garnish with pepper strips, parsley, salad greens, radish roses and Maslinas. Serve with salty rye bread, pumpernickel or crackers. Serves 8 to 12.

CREAMED CHICKEN IN TOAST CUPS (Basic Recipe)

9 slices white bread, crusts removed
melted schmaltz for brushing bread
5 cups diced cooked chicken

1 cup thinly sliced fresh mushrooms
2 tablespoons schmaltz
2 tablespoons flour
salt, pepper and paprika to taste
9 stuffed green olives

Brush trimmed square slices of white bread with melted schmaltz and press them into 3-inch-size muffin pans, greased side down. Brush the inside or sprinkle lightly with some of the melted schmaltz. Bake at 400° for 5 minutes or till lightly browned. Fill centers with mixture of chicken and mushrooms as follows:

Combine diced chicken and sliced mushrooms in a mixing bowl. Brown flour in hot schmaltz in a small saucepan and add ½ cup water or soup stock, chicken and mushrooms. Stir lightly 3 minutes. Add seasonings to taste and fill each of the "bread cups" generously. Bake 8 to 10 minutes at reduced heat, approximately 375°, or till the mushrooms are tender enough to pierce with a toothpick. Do this very carefully so that the mixture in each toast cup will not be disturbed too much. Serve hot with a stuffed olive on top for garnish. Serves 9.

CREAMED SWEETBREADS ON TOAST

8 pairs sweetbreads
cold water to cover
1 tablespoon salt
1 tablespoon lemon juice or vinegar
1/4 cup schmaltz or all-purpose shortening

2 onions, diced fine
6 tablespoons fine cracker crumbs or flour
1 1/2 to 2 cups soup stock
minced parsley
toast points, 4 per serving

Cover sweetbreads with cold water, add salt and lemon juice or vinegar and bring to a quick boil. Skim well, reduce heat and cook over moderate heat approximately 30 minutes or till tender enough to pierce with a fork. Drain well and let cool enough to handle. Remove membrane and dice cooked sweetbreads. Heat schmaltz in a frying pan and brown onions lightly, stirring constantly to prevent scorching. Add cracker crumbs or flour and brown lightly, stirring constantly, then add soup stock and prepared sweetbreads. Cook over low heat for 10 to 15 minutes till well blended. Add minced parsley and serve over toast points arranged on individual plates. Garnish with parsley or sieved hard-cooked egg yolks for color.

Serves 14 to 16.

SNUGGLED BEEFBURGERS

2 cups sifted all-purpose flour
1 teaspoon salt
2 teaspoons baking powder
1/4 teaspoon paprika

1/4 teaspoon poultry seasoning (optional)
1/3 cup oil or vegetable shortening
2/3 cup tomato juice
1/4 cup cold water, approximately

Sift together dry ingredients and stir in oil or cut in vegetable shortening till mixture resembles small peas. Stir in tomato juice, adding water a tablespoonful at a time till a ball of dough is formed. Knead gently on a lightly floured board or cloth for about one minute. Pat or roll out into a rectangle 12 x 8 inches. Spread the meat mixture filling as for jellyroll, roll up and tuck in the ends. Place on a lightly greased baking pan and bake at 375° 30 minutes or till lightly browned. For a glaze, brush top of roll with diluted egg yolk. Serve hot with a thickened tomato sauce or Creole Sauce poured over. Garnish with peas, sliced mushrooms, or a combination of peas and carrots, fresh cooked or frozen, stewed a few minutes and seasoned to taste with salt and pepper.

Filling

1¼ pounds chopped beef	2 eggs
salt and pepper to taste	2 tablespoons crumbs or wheat
1 medium-size onion, grated	germ
1 small carrot, grated	4 tablespoons schmaltz or salad
	oil

Combine all ingredients till well mixed. Heat the schmaltz in a heavy frying pan and turn in the mixture, stirring to brown lightly over moderate heat, about 15 minutes. If too dry, a little soup stock or water may be added to prevent scorching. The meat should be tender. Let cool before spreading this filling.

Serves 6 to 8.

Creole Sauce

2 medium-size onions, diced or	½ cup fresh mushrooms, sliced
sliced	½ cup tomato purée
2 medium-size green peppers,	¼ teaspoon salt
diced fine	a dash of pepper
2 tablespoons shortening	1 teaspoon prepared mustard or
2 tablespoons flour	horseradish

Brown the diced or sliced onions and green peppers in hot melted shortening. Stir in flour, then add remaining ingredients except mustard. Stir while cooking over moderate heat for one minute. Remove from heat and add mustard or horseradish. May be thinned with water or soup stock.

Yields 2 to 2½ cups sauce.

HAMBURGER MUFFIN NESTS (Basic Recipe)

1½ pounds chopped beef	2 tablespoons water or fruit juice
1 teaspoon salt	1 large onion, grated
⅛ teaspoon mixed herb seasoning	1 carrot, grated
(optional)	2 tablespoons wheat germ
2 eggs	(optional)

Grease well the insides of 12 three-inch muffin pans and sprinkle lightly with flour, fine cracker crumbs or matzo meal. Shake to coat well, then invert pans to discard excess flour or other coating. Combine chopped meat with the other listed ingredients, mixing well with fork or fingers to make a smooth mixture. Form 12 balls of equal size and press into muffin pans, making a depression in each. Into the center of each meat muffin place some filling, either before or after baking, as indicated. Serve hot for luncheon or brunch on a bed of cooked spaghetti, macaroni shells, mashed potatoes or steamed rice.

Serves 12.

Filling No. 1

Hard-cooked egg yolks may be mashed, seasoned with salt and pepper or paprika, moistened with a little schmaltz and formed into balls. Place in centers of either unbaked or baked meat muffins. The muffins should be baked 30 to 40 minutes at 375° or till lightly browned. Garnish with a little minced parsley and serve hot.

Filling No. 2

Fill baked muffins with sliced mushrooms and peas, and return to oven for 5 to 10 minutes.

JELLIED LUNCHEON LOAF

Use a 9 x 4½ x 5 inch loaf pan for this molded sandwich main dish. Make white or wholewheat bread sandwiches with any one or all three of the fillings below. Trim off crusts before or after filling, depending on the thickness of sandwiches.

Cheese Spread

1 cup cottage cheese or cream cheese, sieved	3 tablespoons sour cream salt and pepper to taste 3 tablespoons almonds, ground

Combine ingredients with a fork to form a spreadable consistency.

Tuna Fish Spread

1 cupful grated tuna fish 1 teaspoon lemon juice	1 tablespoon mayonnaise 1 hard-cooked egg, chopped fine

Combine till smooth enough to spread on sandwiches, about ½ inch thick.

Hard-Cooked Egg Spread

1 cupful hard-cooked egg, chopped 2 tablespoons mixed pickle relish, finely chopped	1 tablespoon parsley, minced or mixed herb seasoning mayonnaise

Combine till smooth enough to spread, about ¼ inch thick.

Spread two slices of bread with cheese filling; put together and spread the outer surface of one slice. Next spread tuna filling on two slices of bread and put together. Place this sandwich over the one with cheese filling. Make the third sandwich with chopped egg filling, and spread the side of sandwich facing the tuna-filled one. The three sandwiches should now be weighted down for about 30 minutes with a heavy plate. Arrange the rest of the sandwiches the same way, in threes, until you have made enough to stand up inside the loaf pan. Let stand while preparing the gelatin mixture:

TOMATO JUICE GELATIN

2 packages lemon-flavored gelatin	2½ cups thick tomato juice, canned variety
½ cup boiling water	2 tablespoons lemon juice

Dissolve gelatin in boiling water and stir in tomato juice and lemon juice. Pour into lightly buttered loaf pan to a depth of 1 inch. Chill in refrigerator till almost firm, then place sliced pimiento-stuffed olives in any desired design on top of partly jelled tomato juice. Return to refrigerator for 10 minutes, or till set.

Now place the sandwich trios in the pan so that the unspread slices of sandwiches come as close to the narrow sides of pan as possible. The sandwiches may be pressed close together if desired. Now pour in remaining gelatin mixture around and over sandwiches to within ¼ inch of the top of pan. Cover with aluminum foil and chill in the refrigerator till firm, approximately 6 hours.

To unmold, place a flat serving plate or platter over the sandwich loaf in the pan and invert deftly. Let stand at room temperature 5 minutes. Lift off pan. Garnish with salad greens, stuffed olives, deviled eggs, stuffed green pepper rings, etc. Top with swirls of mayonnaise dressing mixed with enough sour cream to enrich but not to thin too much.

To serve, cut with a sharp knife diagonally so that each one-inch sandwich will include part of each type of filled sandwich.

Serves 6 to 8.

MOGEN DOVID LUNCHEON SALAD

4 rounds of bread, thinly sliced, toasted	1 tablespoon sour cream
	shredded lettuce
1 hard-cooked egg, sliced	green pepper slices
3 slices fresh tomato	minced parsley or chopped olives
1 tablespoon mayonnaise	6 thin strips pimiento (canned variety)

Cut sliced rye, pumpernickel, whole wheat or white bread into 2½ inch rounds with a cookie cutter or biscuit cutter. Toast lightly under broiler flame for 1 to 2 minutes, one side only. If many salads are to be prepared, use a cookie sheet for convenience.

Use an egg slicer for the hard-cooked egg so that slices will be even.

Reserve the ends. Place a slice of tomato on one round toasted side, and top with one or two slices of egg. Place the second slice of toast on top, then add the second slice of tomato topped with two egg slices. Place the third round of toast on top, then arrange the next tomato and egg slices and top with the remaining slice of toast. Top with a round end of egg and press together lightly with the fingers. Cover with a towel or aluminum foil to exclude air and let stand about one hour.

When ready to serve, arrange individual salads on serving plates covered with shredded lettuce and make a dressing by combining the mayonnaise with sour cream and spooning it over the pyramid salad so that it runs down the sides. Arrange the green pepper slices and minced parsley around base of salad, then the thin strips of pimiento around to form two crossed triangles, or *Mogen Dovids*. Scatter minced parsley or chopped olives over top and serve. These salads may be prepared in advance, arranged close together and refrigerated till served.

Makes individual serving.

FILLED BEET SALAD RING

2 packages lemon or lime gelatin	2 tablespoons lemon juice
1½ cups boiling hot water	1½ cups grated beets (canned)
1 cup beet liquid (from canned beets)	2 to 4 tablespoons grated horse-radish

Dissolve the gelatin in boiling hot water and as soon as cool add the other ingredients in the order listed. Turn the mixture into a lightly greased or rinsed 10-inch ring mold and chill in the refrigerator overnight. When ready to serve, unmold by quickly dipping bottom of mold in hot water and unmolding at once. By placing a flat serving plate over the mold and inverting while holding plate and mold together firmly, the beet ring will slip out evenly when the mold is lifted from it.

Chill for an hour in the refrigerator before garnishing and filling center with any of the fillings given below.

Serves 10.

Chicken Salad Filling

3 cups finely diced or chopped cooked chicken	3 tablespoons grated raw carrot
½ cup finely diced celery and leaves	½ cup slivered blanched almonds
	½ cup mayonnaise
	¼ cup minced parsley (optional)

Blend together all ingredients.

Chopped Liver Filling

1½ pounds beef or chicken liver
1 onion, diced fine
4 tablespoons schmaltz

4 hard-cooked eggs, chopped
3 tablespoons peanut butter
(optional)
minced parsley (optional)

Broil the liver. Let cool before putting through the food chopper. Brown the diced onion in hot melted schmaltz. Combine with chopped liver, chopped eggs, peanut butter and minced parsley. Season to taste with salt, pepper and paprika. Form into balls the size of hazelnuts. Fill center of Beet Salad Ring.

Pareve Filling

Tuna fish, smoked white fish, salmon or mashed Gefilte Fish may be combined with hard-cooked eggs and mayonnaise dressing to which minced parsley or green pepper may be added for color. Grated raw carrot may substitute for green pepper in the mixture, and strips of green pepper used for garnishing the unmolded Beet Salad Ring.

Any fish used may be flaked or mashed and the hard-cooked eggs, diced or chopped.

Olives, pickles, radish roses, parsley sprigs, green pepper strips, and/or sliced hard-cooked eggs placed three slices together at intervals make attractive garnishes.

Milchig Filling

Dry cottage cheese combined with sour cream, seasoned to taste with salt, pepper and flavor-salt, may be used for filling. Finely diced celery and leaves, green and red pepper finely chopped, and/or pimiento-stuffed green olives sliced thin may be added and also used for garnish.

Egg salad makes an attractive filling. Six to 8 hard-cooked eggs, diced or chopped, seasoned to taste with salt, pepper, flavor-salt and combined with minced green pepper and/or celery and leaves, combined with mayonnaise to which sour cream has been added can be used successfully for filling. Garnish with stuffed (deviled) eggs and greens.

CHICKEN SALAD, QUANTITY TABLES

6 Servings	25 servings	50 servings
1½ cups diced cooked chicken	6 cups	12 cups
1½ cups finely diced celery	6 cups	12 cups
1 cup chopped green pepper	5 cups	10 cups
4 hard-cooked eggs, chopped	15 eggs	30 eggs
½ cup mayonnaise	4 cups (1 quart)	2 quarts
2 tablespoons cider vinegar	½ cup	1 cup
¼ cup minced parsley or watercress	1 cup	2 cups

Note: These ingredients should be combined just before serving time for best results. It is not recommended that salad be stored in the freezer or refrigerator for any length of time.

All measurements are for tightly packed quantities.

Mixtures of equal amounts of diced cooked turkey, goose or capon may be used satisfactorily with cooked chicken. Roast of veal or lamb shoulder may be combined with equal satisfaction with poultry, using $\frac{1}{3}$ to each $\frac{2}{3}$ of the poultry for a good combination.

Serving Chicken Salad

Individual servings on shredded lettuce or in lettuce cups.

Salad rings or mounds may be made by packing the mixed salad tightly in greased ring or mound molds, sprinkling with minced parsley to coat inside of molds if desired. Unmold on beds of salad greens and garnish with strips of red and green peppers, stuffed green olives, radish roses, Maslinas, tiny pickles, sliced tomato and cucumber, etc.

Deviled Eggs, sliced hard-cooked eggs in fan fashion, dusted lightly with paprika or minced parsley make attractive garnishes.

Garnishes That Are Different

CRANBERRY HEARTS

1 can jellied cranberry sauce	8 to 10 thin strips green pepper

Cut the unmolded roll of cranberry sauce into 8 to 10 slices. With a $2\frac{1}{2}$- or 3-inch heart-shaped cookie cutter cut hearts from the slices and lift carefully with a pancake turner to garnish Broiled Spring Chicken halves on individual servings, or arrange around Chicken Salad on serving platter. Place a thin strip of green pepper in each heart to simulate a cupid's dart. If smaller hearts are more suitable, use a cookie cutter $1\frac{1}{2}$ inches in diameter, making 3 hearts from each slice of canned cranberry sauce. Chill the sauce in the can before opening and work rapidly for best results. Or cut the hearts and chill them on a flat plate or platter before using as garnish.

GREEN PEPPER RINGS

Cut off stem and blossom ends from each green pepper so that the rings or slices will be equal in diameter. Remove seeds and fibrous part from peppers, rinse and dry on paper towels. Prepare an egg salad mixture, seasoned to taste, and fill the prepared green peppers compactly.

Chill one hour before slicing into filled rings about ¼ inch thick. Use as a garnish with main dish or salad. If peppers are the three-sectioned kind, the rings will be heart-shaped when stuffed and cut.

JELLIED TOMATO FLOWERPOTS

2 packages lemon- or lime-flavored gelatin
2 cups hot water
2 cups thick tomato sauce (tomato soup, canned)
¼ teaspoon cayenne pepper

pimiento-stuffed olives
tiny pickled gherkins
miniature pickled white onions
½ inch cubes of salami (soft kind)
strips of green pepper and sprigs of parsley

Dissolve gelatin in hot water. Add tomato sauce or canned tomato soup and cayenne pepper, stirring thoroughly. Turn into lightly greased fluted gelatin molds (flowerpot-shaped) or any other with flat bottoms and chill till firm. Unmold and turn each so that the wide or bottom part of molded salad is ready for the "flowers." With plastic toothpicks speared through stuffed olives, gherkins, pickled onions, and salami cubes, stick 3 or 4 of the same or mixed "flowers" into each simulated flowerpot set on individual salad plates and surround with finely minced salad greens and/or parsley sprigs.

Yields 12 to 16.

PINEAPPLE AND CUCUMBER ASPIC SALAD

2 packages lemon- or lime-flavored gelatin
2 cups hot water
1 cup grated cucumber, tightly packed
1¼ cups drained canned crushed pineapple

¼ cup finely chopped nuts
1 small green pepper, chopped fine
¼ cup mayonnaise
3 tablespoons sour cream
3 drops green vegetable coloring

Dissolve gelatin in hot water, then add remaining ingredients in the order listed as soon as gelatin mixture is cool. Turn into lightly greased individual molds and chill overnight or at least 6 hours before unmolding on shredded salad greens. May be turned into large ring mold.

Serves 10 to 12, depending on size of molds.

POND LILIES SALAD

hard-cooked eggs, 1 per serving
mayonnaise dressing, salt, pepper, paprika, minced parsley

salad greens, shredded or chopped and marinated with dressing

With the point of a paring knife cut shelled hard-cooked eggs only through the whites, leaving five or six "petals" attached at one end.

Remove yolks and mash well, adding mayonnaise and seasoning to taste. Form into 1-inch balls, roll in minced parsley and place in the center of each set of "petals" that have been arranged on a bed of salad greens on a large serving plate or platter. Marinate the shredded or chopped mixed greens with French dressing or a mixture of mayonnaise and sour cream if desired. Spears of green pepper may be used for garnish between "pond lilies."

POTATO SALAD DE LUXE

10 potatoes	½ cup minced parsley
1 cup diced celery plus minced leaves	3 hard-cooked eggs, chopped
	3 tablespoons prepared mustard
½ cup minced onion	1 cup salad dressing

Cook potatoes in salted water till tender enough to pierce with a fork. Remove jackets as soon as cool enough to handle. Dice or slice into small pieces. Add remaining ingredients in the order listed, stirring lightly with two forks. Store in glass container in refrigerator till serving time. Arrange in a mound on salad greens and garnish with strips of green and red sweet pepper.

This amount serves 10. Multiply, for the amount required, all ingredients in basic recipe.

CAESAR SALAD

1 large clove garlic	4 tablespoons olive oil
⅛ teaspoon salt	a dash of cayenne or white pepper
2 large heads lettuce	4 tablespoons grated sharp Cheddar-type cheese or Parmesan
1 small bunch chicory and/or Chinese celery cabbage	2 hard-cooked eggs, diced
4 to 6 smoked anchovy fillets	4 tablespoons lemon juice
	3 cups diced white bread, toasted

Use a large salad bowl for mixing and serving this salad. Cut garlic clove in half and rub inside of bowl with cut sides. Sprinkle salt lightly around inside of bowl. Cut lettuce and chicory and/or Chinese celery cabbage (tender spears) with a pair of kitchen scissors into 1- or 1½-inch pieces and drop lightly into bowl. Mash the anchovy fillets to a smooth paste and combine with the oil, cayenne or white pepper, grated cheese and hard-cooked eggs. If preferred, break 3-minute boiled eggs into the salad greens and omit hard-cooked eggs. Add to the salad greens and sprinkle lemon juice over all. Stir lightly with two forks or salad fork and spoon and add the toasted bread cubes while tossing the salad mixture just before serving.

Serves 6 to 8.

CUCUMBER BOATS

Cut medium-size cucumbers in half lengthwise and scoop out to leave shells about ¼ inch thick, or just enough to prevent breakage in handling. The skins may be left on and scored with the teeth of a potato peeler for effect. Chop the seed and center portions of scooped-out cucumbers with green and red peppers, hard-cooked eggs, and/or chopped herring (Herring Salad) for filler of the "boats." A thin slice or two of large black radish may be stuck in to simulate sails. Arrange on shredded salad greens and pass the salad dressing.

Other fillings may be made by combining chopped fresh boiled or frozen green beans, green and red sweet pepper, hard-cooked eggs, sweet mixed pickle relish. Add enough mayonnaise to make a compact filling mixture. Make the sails of cut-out white paper held in place with colored toothpicks.

Fleishig fillings may be combinations of chopped chicken, turkey or beef, lamb or veal roast put through the grinder the second time with hard-cooked eggs. Add minced parsley or bits of fresh dill, and enough mayonnaise to hold the ingredients together.

Milchig fillings: Equal parts of cottage cheese and sour cream, adding minced parsley, chopped nuts of any kind, and/or chopped chives or green onions with salt and white pepper to taste.

Cream cheese combined with grated Cheddar-type cheese and a little sour cream may be substituted for cottage cheese.

TORAH SCROLL SANDWICHES

Cut away crusts from square slices of white bread. Place these close together on an aluminum foil-covered table or ironing board and pass a heated iron over to press thin as well as heat through. Have the filling to be used ready and an assistant to spread each slice of bread deftly before rolling up and tying with 6-inch lengths of white and light blue ribbon. When filled, rolled, and tied with ribbon, place close together in an aluminum foil lined cardboard box. These can be prepared hours in advance or the night before and refrigerated.

It is best to "iron" 8 to 10 slices of bread at a time so that these can be rolled easily while warm. They will hold their shape if tied quickly after filling and rolling. Or place as many "scrolls" together as can be handled easily and wrap tightly in aluminum foil for refrigerating till needed.

Fillings: Ground sausage of any kind with an equal amount of hard-cooked egg, mashed or chopped, and moistened with mayonnaise dressing. Seasoning may be added if desired. Chopped chicken or beef liver with peanut butter and minced parsley. Mashed sardines with hard-cooked eggs, moistened with French dressing to make a smooth paste. Chopped herring, grated apple and ground almonds, moistened with mayonnaise to make a smooth filling.

One cup of prepared filling will be sufficient for 6 to 8 sandwich rolls or scrolls.

CALLA LILY SANDWICHES

60 slices white bread (from large
    sandwich loaf)

Trim off crusts. Place 6 to 8 slices at a time on an aluminum foil-covered ironing board, in two rows, close together. Heat an electric iron and pass it over the sliced bread, pressing down to flatten as well as warm the bread through. Roll each slice as rapidly as possible into a cornucopia or cala lily shape, fastening with a toothpick. When all are shaped, place them in the refrigerator, wrapped in aluminum foil or a double towel, until ready for fillings.

Prepare the filling mixtures and store in the refrigerator until about 30 minutes before guests are expected. Below are three suggested fillings, one pink, one pale green and one pale yellow, each sufficient for filling 20 Calla Lily Sandwiches. If more variety is desired, use the three additional fillings we have listed. These six fillings can, of course, be used in any way you wish, as a sandwich or canapé spread.)

Have some thin strips of green peppers ready to insert, making the Calla Lily complete. Garnishes may be olives, tiny pickles, etc.

Work rapidly, preferably with an assistant.

Pink Filling

2 eight-ounce cans of tuna fish
    (or salmon)
1 canned pimiento pepper, mashed
1 tablespoon ketchup

2 tablespoons mayonnaise
2 hard-cooked eggs, mashed
2 tablespoons mixed pickle relish
    (optional)

Mash the fish thoroughly, then add other ingredients in the order listed. Work together to make a smooth, compact filling. If not the desired tone of pink, add a few drops of vegetable coloring and mix well. Store in a glass-covered dish.

Pale Green Filling

1 pound cream cheese	¼ teaspoon salt
4 tablespoons finely ground pistachio nuts	4 teaspoons sugar
4 tablespoons finely ground almonds	4 tablespoons sour cream or whipped cream
	3 to 4 drops green vegetable coloring.

Mash the cheese, then add remaining ingredients to make a smooth filling mixture. Chill before using.

Yellow Filling

10 to 12 hard-cooked eggs	a dash of powdered garlic
1 teaspoon salt	3 to 4 tablespoons each mayonnaise and sour cream
a dash of white pepper	3 tablespoons finely minced parsley

Mash the eggs thoroughly to a smooth mixture, then add remaining ingredients in the order listed, mixing well. Add 2 or 3 drops of yellow vegetable coloring to make the desired shade. Chill before using.

Chopped Corned Beef or Smoked Tongue Filling

3 cups finely ground meat	3 tablespoons mayonnaise
6 hard-cooked eggs, mashed	3 tablespoons chopped pickle relish
3 tablespoons minced parsley	

Combine by mixing thoroughly. Chill before using as filling.

Chopped Cooked Chicken or Turkey Filling

3 cups finely ground cooked poultry, packed	a dash of cayenne pepper (optional)
4 hard-cooked eggs, mashed	4 tablespoons finely chopped green pepper
¼ cup chopped almonds or other nuts	4 tablespoons mayonnaise

Combine ingredients in the order listed. Chill before using.

STAR SANDWICHES

With a cookie cutter of six-pointed star shape, cut thin slices of equal number of white and rye or pumpernickel bread. Put together with any smooth sandwich filling. Wrap in aluminum foil and refrigerate till serving time. Serve with cocktails, wine or fruit punch. Allow 4 per serving.

Fillings may be mixtures of cream cheese and smoked sardines, well mashed and seasoned with a few drops of lemon juice and/or pepper to taste. Or equal parts cream cheese and sharp Cheddar-type cheese, moistened with a little sour cream or mayonnaise. Or ground-up smoked tongue or pastrami, moistened with mayonnaise to make a smooth paste. Chopped liver and peanut butter make a good filling. Minced parsley may be added to any of these mixtures.

Sweet fillings may be any combination of cream cheese and fruit preserves with a little grated orange or lemon rind added. Or cream cheese with finely ground almonds, brazil nuts, filberts or walnuts and sweetened with jam or honey to taste.

Star sandwiches may be decorated by spearing tiny sweet-sour gherkins, pimiento olives, candied fruits or canned well-drained cherries with a plastic toothpick into centers or at an angle.

TORAH SCROLL CAKE (Open Book Cake)

Make a double recipe of your favorite cake mixture. Turn it into an aluminum-lined cake pan, at least 1 inch deep, any size from 12 x 18 to the size that will fit into your oven.

Bake and let cool before decorating with frosting, in white with blue, or blue with white lettering, giving the date and name of the celebrant. The borders of cake may be shaped to resemble a scroll, or left uncut, with the frosting marking the outline of a scroll.

Where the services of a professional baker or caterer are available, the cake may be made as elaborate as the budget permits.

Another popular idea in vogue is to make the cake in the form of an open book, with lettering and border to suit the taste, and in keeping with the occasion. For this two rectangular cakes may be baked and fitted together before frosting and decorating, so that the center forms the meeting of both pages.

A little ingenuity on the part of the home baker will no doubt result in personalized cakes to the delight of celebrant as well as guests.

Follow directions on the package of confectioners' sugar for making both the frosting and the ornamental mixtures. Use a cake decorator or a small pastry tube for best results.

SCRIPTURE CAKE

Fruit cake may have originated in pre-Biblical days. At least the idea of fruit cake dates back to ancient days when little cakes were made by pressing together various dried fruits such as raisins, dates, figs, dried plums and apricots, forming round flat cakes. Mention is made in Samuel I-XXX-12, also in Samuel II-XVI-1 of such "fruit cake."

There is a story about a certain cake which developed somewhere in New England many, many years ago. It was first made as a contribution for a contest at a county or village fair. The woman who made it called it Scripture Cake and appended a list of the ingredients, with Biblical citations. It became very popular, although to this day the woman who created it has remained "unheralded and unsung." It was referred to by ministers and lay preachers as the shining example of how "even the humblest occupation," home-baking, could be spiritually ennobling. Anyone who would bake a Scripture Cake would of necessity have to know the Bible well, for the recipe or "receipt" was always written out as follows:

1 cup butter	(Judges–5:25)	Milk
2 cups sugar	(Jeremiah–6:20)	Sweet cane from a far place
3½ cups flour	(I Kings–5:2)	Solomon's provisions
2 cups figs	(I Samuel–30:12)	Cake of pressed figs
2 cups raisins	(I Samuel–30:12)	Two clusters of raisins
1 cup water	(Genesis–24:22)	Drinking by camels
1 cup almonds	(Genesis–43:11)	Almonds
6 eggs	(Isaiah–10:14)	As one gathered eggs
a little salt	(Leviticus–2:13)	Every meal seasoned with salt
1 tablespoon honey	(Exodus–16:31)	Manna described like wafers made with honey
spices to taste	(I Kings–10:2)	Sheba came with spices

Directions for mixing cake: Follow Solomon's advice for making good boys (Proverbs–23:14) —*Beat well.*

To put the ingredients together, cream butter and sugar in a large mixing bowl. Stir in half the amount of sifted flour till smooth. Chop figs and raisins and cook in a cup of cold water for 5 minutes, then cool while blanching and chopping the almonds. Beat egg yolks, stir in honey. Beat egg whites with a pinch of salt till stiff enough to hold a peak. Combine the yolk and honey alternately with remainder of flour, then stir in beaten egg whites lightly, adding a dash of ground cinnamon or allspice. Beat in accordance with "King Solomon's directions" for "making good boys." Use an electric mixer, if possible. Turn the cake batter into a large rectangular cake pan that has been lined with aluminum foil or waxpaper and bake 50 minutes at 325° or till lightly browned on top and the sides of cake begin to stand away from sides of pan. Cool before cutting into 2-inch squares or diamond shapes.

Serves 10 to 12.

BRIDAL WREATH COFFEE RING

¼ cup butter or substitute	½ teaspoon salt
½ cup sugar	⅓ cup butter or substitute
2 tablespoons orange juice	⅔ cup milk or orange juice
1 tablespoon grated orange rind	2 tablespoons melted shortening
12 candied cherries	½ cup fine cookie crumbs
60 blanched almond halves	½ cup dark brown sugar
12 strips citron, green colored	½ teaspoon cinnamon
1¾ cups sifted flour	¼ cup finely ground or chopped
3 teaspoons baking powder	almonds

Spread butter or substitute over bottom and sides of a 9-inch ring mold or well cake pan with removable rim. Pat sugar into the melted butter and sprinkle lightly with orange rind and juice (or water). Arrange candied cherries and almond halves to form blossoms, 5 almonds around each cherry, and place a strip of green colored citron for stem on each of the 12 flowers. Use bowl of a teaspoon to press the flowers down into the pan.

Sift together flour, baking powder and salt in a bowl and cut in shortening with two knives or pastry blender till it resembles coarse cornmeal. Stir in the liquid to form a ball of dough. Turn out on a lightly floured board or cloth and knead gently a few minutes. Roll into a rectangle 12 x 8 inches and brush with melted butter or substitute. Sprinkle with cookie crumbs, brown sugar and cinnamon, then ground almonds, and roll up from the long side jellyroll fashion. Cut into 12 slices and place cut side down in the pan over the "flowers" of cherries and almond halves. Press down lightly with the bowl of mixing spoon and bake 35 to 40 minutes at 400° or till lightly browned on top. Let stand in the pan 3 to 5 minutes before unmolding on a serving plate or platter.

Yields 12 wreaths in ring.

CHOCOLATE CAKE SUPREME

3 cups sifted cake flour	1 cup sugar
3 teaspoons baking powder	3 eggs
½ teaspoon salt	2 tablespoons grated orange rind
¾ cup shortening	¼ cup orange marmalade
	1 cup orange juice

Sift together cake flour, baking powder and salt. Cream shortening and sugar till light and fluffy, then add one egg at a time, beating well after each addition. Stir in orange rind and marmalade. Combine the two mixtures by adding the dry ingredients to the creamed mixture alternately with orange juice, a little at a time, till well blended. Turn into a well-greased rectangular cake pan, 10 x 15 x 1, and bake 30 minutes at 350°. When cool, cut cake into squares and spread with frosting, or serve with chocolate sauce poured over each cut.

Chocolate Sauce

1 package semi-sweet chocolate bits (1 cup)	4 tablespoons hot milk if used for frosting, or
2 tablespoons butter or substitute	½ cup hot milk if used for sauce
1½ cups sifted confectioners' sugar	1 teaspoon vanilla

Put chocolate bits in top of double boiler, add butter or substitute, place over hot water till melted, stirring till smooth. For frosting, remove from heat and add sugar and milk, stirring till of spreadable consistency, adding the flavoring a few drops at a time during the stirring. For sauce, increase the milk to ½ cupful and proceed as above.

Serves 30.

FEATHERLIGHT LEMON CAKE

1 cup sifted cake flour	1 teaspoon cream of tartar
½ cup sugar	1 cup sugar
1 cup egg whites (6 or 7)	1 teaspoon vanilla
½ teaspoon salt	1 tablespoon grated lemon rind
	4 egg yolks

Sift together the sifted flour and sugar three times into a large mixing bowl. Place egg whites in another mixing bowl and add salt and cream of tartar. Beat egg whites till frothy, then add cup of sugar gradually while beating with a rotary beater till stiff. Add flavoring and fold in the flour and sugar mixture gradually, using an over and over motion till thoroughly smooth. Add the grated lemon rind, then the beaten yolks, and fold into the batter. Pour the mixture into an ungreased 10-inch tube pan and bake 1 hour and 10 minutes at 325°. Remove from oven and invert the cake-in-pan until cold. Hang the inverted pan over a funnel or rest it between two inverted cake pans so that air will circulate under the cake till cold. Spread with the following frosting:

Lemon Frosting

4 egg yolks	⅓ cup lemon juice
⅔ cup sugar	1 tablespoon grated lemon rind
	½ cup heavy cream, beaten stiff

Beat egg yolks till thick and add sugar gradually while continuing to beat till lemon-colored. Use the top of a double boiler for this. Add lemon juice, place over boiling water and cook over moderate heat, stirring constantly till thickened. Stir in grated rind and remove from heat till cold. Or chill in refrigerator. When cold, fold this mixture into beaten cream and spread lightly in swirls over top of cake.

Serves 8 to 10.

GRAHAM CRACKER CHIFFON CAKE

2¼ cups sifted cake flour	¾ cup cold water or fruit juice
1¾ cup sugar	2 teaspoons vanilla
3 teaspoons baking powder	5 egg yolks
1 teaspoon salt	1 cup egg whites (7 or 8)
½ cup salad oil	½ teaspoon cream of tartar
	2 cups fine graham cracker crumbs

Sift together flour, sugar, baking powder and salt into a large mixing bowl. Make a well in the center and add oil, liquid, flavoring and egg yolks. Beat till smooth with an electric beater or other rotary beater. Beat egg white with cream of tartar till it forms stiff peaks and fold into the first mixture with a spatula or fork till blended. Do not beat or stir too long. Sprinkle the graham cracker crumbs over the batter a little at a time, folding in gently after each addition. Pour batter into an un-greased 10-inch tube cake pan. Bake 55 minutes at 325°, then increase heat to 350° for the next 12 to 15 minutes or till the cake is lightly browned on top and has risen evenly to top of cake pan.

This cake should be about 4 inches high when baked. Invert at once over a heavy funnel so that air circulates under and around cake and let hang till cold. If no heavy funnel is handy, use a couple of inverted cake pans and rest inverted cake in the pan so that air circulates. Frost top and sides as desired.

Serves 12 to 18.

Variation 1: When cake is cold, use a long-bladed thin knife to cut a larger hole in the center and put in a quart container of ice cream just before serving time. Use a bowl spoon for serving a ball of the ice cream with each cut of cake.

Variation 2: Fill center with whipped cream, sweetened to taste and flavored with rum or cherry cordial.

MOCHA SPICE CAKE

1¾ cups sifted all-purpose flour	½ cup vegetable shortening
2 teaspoons baking powder	¾ cup sugar
⅛ teaspoon salt	⅓ cup dark brown sugar, tightly
¼ teaspoon each allspice, nutmeg and cinnamon	packed
	2 eggs, beaten
½ teaspoon instant coffee or sub-stitute	¾ cup milk

Sift together into a mixing bowl the first five dry ingredients. Cream shortening and add sugar gradually while mixing to a soft and fluffy consistency, then work in the dark brown sugar till light and fluffy. Add well-beaten eggs and blend well. Stir sifted dry ingredients into this mixture alternately with the milk till well blended and pour into 2 greased 8-inch layer cake pans. Bake 25 minutes at 375°. When cool, put together with the following filling and top with slightly thinned filling put on in swirls.

Filling and Topping

¼ cup softened butter or substitute	few grains of salt
2 cups confectioners' sugar, sifted	1 tablespoon instant coffee or sub-
3 tablespoons milk	stitute
	½ teaspoon vanilla

Combine the softened shortening with confectioners' sugar by stirring with a fork, adding a little milk at a time and working in the salt, instant coffee and vanilla in the final strokes to form a smooth enough mixture to spread easily with a spatula. After filling the cake, add a few more drops of milk at a time to the mixture till it can be spooned over top of cake in a swirl pattern.

Serves 8.

PINEAPPLE MERINGUE CAKE

½ cup butter	5 tablespoons milk
1½ cups sugar	1 teaspoon vanilla
4 eggs, separated	1 can crushed pineapple, No. 2
1 cup sifted cake flour	size
1 teaspoon baking powder	1 cup heavy cream, whipped
	¼ teaspon almond extract

Cream butter and add sugar a little at a time while creaming till well blended and until half the amount of sugar has been used. Add egg yolks and mix well. Sift together flour and baking powder into the creamed mixture, adding a little milk at a time while stirring to a smooth batter. Spread this batter evenly in two layer cake pans that have been greased and lined with waxpaper, or with aluminum foil, then greased. Use removable bottom pans if possible.

Beat egg whites stiff, adding a little sugar at a time of the remaining amount while continuing to beat till the mixture is stiff enough to hold a peak. Add vanilla a few drops at a time, folding in carefully. Spread each layer of batter in the pans with the meringue and bake 40 minutes at 350° or till the meringue is lightly browned on top. Cool the two layers of cake while preparing the filling as follows:

Drain syrup from the crushed pineapple. Use a fruit press if possible. (Use the syrup for pudding sauce or as a glaze for poultry, duck especially. Or utilize it in a cooling drink.) Fold the well-drained crushed pineapple into whipped cream, adding a few drops at a time of the almond extract. Turn out one layer of baked cake, meringue-side up, on a cake plate, spread on the pineapple-whipped cream filling and top with the other layer, meringue-side up. Chill in the refrigerator 1 hour before serving.

Serves 10.

GLAZED UPSIDE-DOWNIES

1 cup sugar	¼ teaspoon salt
½ cup butter or vegetable short-ening	1 cup milk or fruit juice
	1 teaspoon vanilla
2 eggs, separated	4 tablespoons melted shortening
2 cups sifted flour	1 cup dark brown sugar
2 teaspoons baking powder	16 dried apricot halves
	16 pecan halves

Cream sugar and butter or shortening. Add egg yolks and beat till smooth. Sift together flour, baking powder and salt. Stir into the creamed mixture alternately with the liquid and vanilla flavoring. Beat egg whites and fold in. Grease 16 muffin cups, 2-inch size, and place a tablespoon of brown sugar into each pan. Place a dried apricot half over a pecan half in each, then fill two-thirds full with the batter. Bake 20 to 25 minutes at 350° or till lightly browned. Turn out while hot on a flat plate or platter that has been dusted lightly with confectioners' sugar. The brown sugar over nut and fruit will form a glaze as the cakes cool.

Yields 16.

COOKIE DOUGH-LINED CHEESECAKE

1 cup sifted flour	5 drops vanilla
¼ cup sugar	1 egg yolk
1 teaspoon grated lemon rind	½ cup butter or substitute

Combine flour, sugar, grated rind and vanilla in a mixing bowl. Make a well in the center and add egg yolk and butter. Work together till blended, using a pastry blender or fingers to form a ball of dough. Wrap in aluminum foil and chill in the refrigerator about 1 hour. Roll out to ⅛-inch thickness and place in a well-buttered 9- or 10-inch spring form cake pan, pressing it lightly to fit over bottom and up sides of pan as far as it will reach—about 3 inches all the way around. Bake 20 minutes at 400° or till a light golden brown in color. Let cool before turning in the cheese filling.

Cheese Filling

2½ pounds cream cheese	1 teaspoon grated lemon rind
1½ cups sugar	¼ teaspoon vanilla
3 tablespoons flour	5 eggs
2 teaspoons grated orange rind	2 egg yolks
	¼ cup heavy whipping cream

Combine cheese, sugar, flour and grated fruit rinds in a mixing bowl. Stir in vanilla and whole eggs one at a time, stirring lightly after each addition. Add the 2 egg yolks with the heavy cream, folding in as lightly as possible. Turn the cheese mixture into the baked crust inside of cake pan and bake 12 to 15 minutes at 550°. Reduce heat to 225° and bake 1 hour longer. Leave in the oven with oven door open for one hour or till cold. Remove from oven. Let stand at least an hour before cutting and serving.

Serves 10 to 12.

Variation: Bake bottom lining of cake first. Then line sides. Fill with mixture and bake.

CRACKER CRUMB TORTE

14 graham crackers	9 tablespoons sugar
9 eggs, separated	1 lemon, grated rind and juice

Roll crackers in a paper bag till reduced to powder. Sift. Beat egg yolks till lemon-colored and creamy, adding sugar gradually while beating thoroughly by hand or in electric mixer. Add grated rind of lemon and strained juice. Beat another few strokes. Beat egg whites stiff and fold in last. Turn into 2 well-buttered and flour-dusted 9-inch layer cake pans and bake at 350° for 30 minutes or till set and lightly browned. When cool, put layers together with the following filling and frosting.

Mocha-Cream Frosting and Filling

1 cup heavy cream, whipped	2 tablespoons dry cocoa, sifted with
2 tablespoons confectioners' sugar and	1 tablespoon soluble coffee or Postum
	1 teaspoon rum or vanilla extract

Combine whipped cream with the sifted ingredients. Beat in flavoring till the mixture is of spreadable consistency. Use for filling and frosting.

Sprinkle with sifted graham cracker crumbs and finely ground walnuts, in an inch-wide border on top of cake, or in wheel spoke design.

Serves 8 to 10.

APRICOT JAM GEMS

4 cups sifted flour	2 tablespoons heavy cream or
1 cup butter or substitute	evaporated milk
1 cup sugar	1 teaspoon vanilla
½ teaspoon salt	1 teaspoon brandy
4 eggs, separated	½ cup chopped almonds or walnuts
	1 8-ounce glass of apricot jam

Combine flour, butter, sugar (reserving 2 tablespoonfuls), salt, in a large mixing bowl. Use a wire pastry blender or fingers to blend till small crumbs are formed. Add egg yolks, cream and flavorings and mix with a spoon till well blended. Roll out on a lightly floured board or pastry cloth to ⅛-inch thickness or thinner and cut into triangles, diamond shapes or rounds. Or use any fancy-shaped cutter. Brush the cookies with lightly beaten egg whites and sprinkle with chopped nuts combined with remaining reserved sugar. Bake on buttered cookie sheets 8 to 10 minutes at 350° or till lightly browned. Remove cookies when cold and put two together with a bit of apricot jam. Or place a bit of the jam in the center of each cookie and sprinkle with more of the nut and sugar mixture.

Yields about 100 cookies, or 50 "gems."

FLOWER FRITTERS

2 cups all-purpose flour	6 tablespoons rum or sherry
½ teaspoon salt	melted shortening for frying
3 egg yolks	½ cup confectioners' sugar
3 tablespoons cream	1 egg white
1 tablespoon sugar	raspberry or cherry preserves, as
	required

Sift flour and salt into mixing bowl. Add egg yolks, cream, sugar and rum or sherry, stirring to combine into a ball of dough. Knead on a lightly floured board or pastry cloth till the dough no longer sticks to hand or board. Let stand at room temperature for 20 to 30 minutes before rolling out to ⅛-inch thickness. Use three sizes of cookie cutters or thin glasses for cutting rounds. Brush a large circle with egg white and place the next size circle on. Brush with egg white before pressing on the smallest circle. Press lightly, just enough to make the rounds of dough stick together.

Have the shortening hot enough to brown a cube of bread in one minute. Use a heavy frying pan. With a spatula life each triple-decker into the hot fat and let cook over moderate heat till lightly browned and curled at the edges, resembling a flower. Skim out with a slotted spoon or perforated pancake turner. Place each on a paper-lined flat plate as you lift from pan. Do not crowd the "flowers" while cooking in fat. When all have been cooked and cooled, place a tiny bit of preserves—raspberry or cherry—in the centers. Or dust lightly with confectioners' sugar before serving.

Yield depends on size of flowers.

PUFF PASTE (called Blätter-teig)

½ pound butter or margarine	½ teaspoon cream of tartar
2 cups sifted flour	⅔ cup ice water

Cut the butter or margarine into inch pieces and toss in a little flour to coat all sides. Sift together the flour and cream of tartar. Sift a little at a time over the floured bits of butter while working together with a fork until it forms large chunks. Add a little ice water at a time while continuing to work the mixture together into a ball of dough. Wrap in aluminum foil and chill in the refrigerator at least 30 minutes.

Roll out on a lightly floured board or cloth to ⅛-inch thickness for most pastries, thicker if desired for filling.

For extra flakiness, roll the dough into a rectangle about ¼-inch thick, 12 x 16 inches, keeping the corners as square as possible. Keep enough flour on the kneading board to prevent streaks of the butter from sticking. Fold over to make three thicknesses of pastry, right side over to center, then left side over. Brush off excess flour and roll out into the same size rectangle, folding into thirds. Again dust off excess flour and roll out for the third time into the same size rectangle. Wrap up and chill for 30 minutes. Roll out for the fourth and final time into the same size rectangle, fold over as before. Chill till ready for baking, at least 1 hour or overnight. Roll out as required for the particular pastry.

PUFF PASTE DELICACIES

Cream Filling

⅓ cup sugar	3 eggs, beaten well
3 tablespoons cornstarch	3 cups scalded milk
1 tablespoon flour	1 teaspoon vanilla
	¼ teaspoon almond flavoring

Combine the dry ingredients and stir into the well-beaten eggs till smooth. Add scalded milk gradually while stirring till smooth. Cook in top of double boiler, stirring constantly until mixture thickens, about 10 minutes. Remove from heat and stir in vanilla and almond flavoring.

Stir constantly to prevent film from forming on top of the mixture. This cream filling may be stored in a covered glass jar in the refrigerator to use as required.

Yields 3½ cups.

Jam Baskets

½ the amount of Puff Paste	currant or red raspberry jam
¾ cup Cream Filling	¼ cup finely chopped nuts

Roll out Puff Paste to ¼-inch thickness. Cut into rounds 3 inches in diameter, making 12 circles. With a small round cutter or thin cordial glass cut out 1½-inch rounds from the centers of 6 rounds. Moisten the whole rounds with a little milk or fruit juice and top with the cut-out rounds, making 6 "baskets." Place these on a baking pan and chill 30 minutes, then bake 5 minutes at 450°, reducing heat to 350° and baking 15 to 20 minutes longer. Cool on a wire rack. Split the shells or baskets about ¼ inch from bottom and spread lower part with cream filling. Replace the cut-out top and fill center with jam, topping with chopped nuts.

Sweethearts

½ recipe Puff Paste	12 large blanched almonds
1½ cups Cream Filling	whipped cream topping

Roll out Puff Paste to ¼-inch thickness and cut out 12 hearts with a cutter. Place these on an ungreased cookie sheet or baking pan and chill in the refrigerator about 30 minutes. Bake 5 minutes at 450° then reduce heat to 350° for the next 15 to 20 minutes or till lightly browned. Cool on a wire rack. Split each heart pastry and put together with some of the Cream Filling. Top with a pair of almond halves arranged to resemble twin hearts. Top with whipped cream fluted through a pastry tube around the rim of the heart pastries.

Uncooked Almond Filling or Topping

2 tablespoons butter or margarine	1 egg yolk
¼ cup sugar	1½ tablespoons good rum
	½ cup ground blanched almonds

Work the butter or margarine in a bowl till creamy, then add sugar gradually while beating with a fork till creamy and fluffy. Add egg yolk and beat well. Stir in rum and finely ground almonds.

Yields ⅔ cup filling or topping.

Peachies

Roll Puff Paste into a rectangle ¼ inch in thickness and cut out 12 rounds 3 inches in diameter. Place these on a baking sheet and chill 30 minutes. Bake 5 minutes at 450°, then reduce heat to 350° for 15 to 20 minutes. Let cool on a wire rack. Split each of the rounds in two without crumbling. Place a well-drained canned peach half cut side down on each of the rounds. Place a few dots of the Almond Filling around the peach, brush with a little of the Cream Filling for a glaze and return to oven for 5 minutes at 350°. Let cool on the baking sheet before removing to serving plates.

Spirals or Pattie Shells

Roll out Puff Paste into a rectangle ⅛ inch thick. Cut into ½-inch strips, then cut strips as required. Form circles or spirals, or double spirals (like letter *S*, tightly rolled). Brush with diluted egg yolk and chill on the cookie sheet for 30 minutes before baking 5 minutes at 450°; reduce heat to 350° for 12 to 15 minutes. When cold, top with a little Almond Filling, pressed in centers of spirals or circles.

Arrange strips to form a three-tier pattie shell. Bake as above. When cold, fill centers with fresh or frozen blueberries, strawberries, raspberries and top with whipped cream and chopped nuts, just before serving.

Stars of David

Cut thinly rolled out Puff Paste into ½-inch-wide strips. Cut 5-inch lengths and arrange triangles, placing one triangle over another one to form a *Mogen Dovid*. Press together lightly and brush with fruit juice or diluted egg yolk for a glaze. Sprinkle with chopped nuts or colored sugar. Evaporated milk makes a good glaze for tops of any of the above pastries. Bake as directed.

CREAM PUFFS

⅓ cup butter	4 eggs
⅔ cup milk	½ cup whipping cream for filling
⅔ cup sifted flour	¼ teaspoon vanilla
¼ teaspoon salt	2 tablespoons confectioners' sugar

Heat butter and milk in top of double boiler. When blended, dump in the flour and salt all at once and stir vigorously until the mixture forms a ball of dough that stands away from sides of pan. Keep the water underneath boiling during this process. Remove from heat and beat in one egg at a time till smooth and glossy. Drop from a tablespoon onto a greased baking pan and bake 40 minutes at 450° or till lightly browned and puffed high. Let cool. Beat cream till thick enough to hold a peak, working in the confectioners' sugar and vanilla a little at a time. Cut a slit in side or top of each cream puff and fill generously.

Yields 12.

Variation: Fill with Cream Filling as in Puff Paste.

PLUMPED DRIED FRUITS

Apricots, pitted dates (unsugared), figs (black mission), prunes that have been soaked and pitted can be used to advantage for serving at various celebrations in the home. The older generation of celebrants is most appreciative of this easy-to-munch fare.

Place dried apricots, figs and prunes in a colander and pour boiling water over all. Let drain into a large pan so that the steam will rise and soften the fruits in the colander. Placing a cover over the colander is suggested to hasten this process. Let stand 30 to 45 minutes. Repeat if apricots and figs are still hard.

Dates that are unsugared should be pitted and placed on a plate at room temperature for drying before filling or rolling in confectioners' sugar. Prunes that have been steamed in the colander may be dried between paper towels, then cut into with the point of a paring knife and pits removed. Or soak large prunes overnight and drain thoroughly. They should be puffed and easy to open for removal of pits. Drain or dry well before stuffing or rolling in confectioners' sugar and/or ground almonds.

FONDANT FILLING FOR DRIED FRUITS (Basic Recipe)

1 pound confectioners' sugar
⅛ pound butter or vegetable shortening
a few drops of almond flavoring

1 tablespoon sherry
1 tablespoon evaporated milk or cream (any fruit juice may be substituted)

Combine with a fork in the order listed to make a smooth fondant thick enough to hold its shape when used for filling prepared dried fruits.

SALTED ALMONDS

1 pound shelled almonds
boiling water to cover
4 tablespoons melted butter or vegetable shortening

½ teaspoon salt
1 teaspoon almond flavoring or vanilla

Let almonds stand in the hot water, well covered, for 5 to 8 minutes. Drain and remove brown peeling. Dry with a paper towel and spread almonds on a cookie sheet. Drizzle with the melted shortening used and sprinkle with salt. Bake 5 minutes at 350° on top shelf of oven or till the nuts are lightly browned. Sprinkle while hot with the flavoring, shake the pan or stir nuts with a fork. Let cool before serving in bon bon dishes.

SPICED NUTS

½ cup sugar	¼ teaspoon salt
¼ teaspoon cinnamon	2 tablespoons cold water
¼ teaspoon nutmeg or cloves	1 cup nut halves—blanched almonds, pecans, walnuts

Combine all ingredients except nuts and bring to a boil in a saucepan over moderate heat. Reduce heat and let syrup simmer till it reaches the soft-ball stage—when a drop in cold water remains a soft ball between the fingers—235° by cooking thermometer. Blanch the almonds by covering with boiling water, letting stand under cover for 5 to 8 minutes. Pour off water and remove skins. Dry between paper towels and drop into the syrup. Stir till the nut meats are well covered with the syrup. Remove at once from heat and turn the mixture into a shallow pan, spreading the glazed nuts apart with a fork or knife point. Break apart when cold. Pecans and walnut halves should be treated in the same manner for syrup glaze. Serve in bon bon dishes.

ISRAEL DAY CELEBRATIONS

Since the establishment of the new Republic of Israel on May 14th, 1948 (5th of Iyar of the Hebrew Calendar), it has become customary to celebrate ISRAEL DAY. In Israel it is a legal holiday, with appropriate public celebrations in remote agricultural settlements as well as in the large cities.

Jews the world over have added this most recent holiday to the calendar of holidays and festivals. It has become customary to serve some favorite Israeli foods at such celebrations.

While a characteristic cuisine is still in the process of development in Israel, some foods are commonly associated with the new state. One such favorite is the highly spiced "falafel" which is to Israel what the "hot dog" and "grilled hamburger" are to Americans.

"Falafel" is sold at open roadside stands, in market places as well as in city eateries. It is eaten out of hand, hot and spicy, with a freshly baked flat roll called *peetah* wrapped about it for easy handling.

Because traditional favorites are native berries and small fruits, nuts and citrus fruits, raisins and almonds, dates, figs, dried fruits, such as apricots, prunes and pears, these are customary "kibbet."

Fruit soups, cooked and uncooked, hot or chilled, are commonly served as meal-starters. Native vegetables, from eggplant to okra and squash, combined in various ways with tomatoes, form many of the main dishes. Fish, meat and poultry dishes take their place on the Sabbath and holiday menu in accordance with family customs of recent immigrants from various countries.

"HOT" FALAFEL

4 cups thick purée of cooked
    chick peas (*nahit*)
1 teaspoon salt
½ teaspoon white pepper
½ teaspoon hot red pepper or 1
    mashed pickled red pepper
½ teaspoon mixed herbs (basil,
    marjoram, thyme, etc.)

¼ cup fine cracker or bread
    crumbs
4 eggs
4 tablespoons melted vegetable
    shortening or olive oil (Tahini)
1 cup dry crumbs
deep melted shortening for frying

Canned chick peas may be drained and mashed. Or, soak dry chick peas overnight in cold water to cover. Drain and rinse. Add cold water to cover and cook till tender enough to mash between thumb and fore-finger. Using a pressure cooker lessens the time of preparation. Follow directions for using your pressure cooker. When the chick peas are tender, drain and put through the fine blade of the food chopper to form a thick purée. Add salt and other seasonings to taste. Stir in cracker crumbs and eggs, mixing well till combined. Work in the 4 tablespoons melted short-ening or oil last. Form into 2½- or 3-inch "fingers," not more than an inch in diameter, and roll each in dry crumbs. When all are formed, drop into hot melted shortening or oil, in a frying basket if possible, and fry till nicely browned on all sides. Turn carefully with a long handled fork if necessary. Lift out of frying basket and drain well before serving hot. Can be reheated in a warm oven.

Yields 36 to 40.

SWEET FALAFEL (American version of Hot Falafel)

Substitute ½ cup sugar for the white and hot pepper. Add 1 teaspoon mixed sweet herbs (thyme, marjoram, basil, etc.), 2 tablespoons lemon juice and 1 tablespoon grated lemon rind.

Combine the ingredients as in Hot Falafel and form into balls an inch in diameter or smaller. Roll these in crumbs and fry till nicely browned. If desired, dust lightly with confectioners' sugar while hot. Spear with colored toothpicks for easy serving.

Add ¼ cup finely ground almonds for variation.

PEETAH

These flat rolls are baked fresh for every serving with family meals or as wrap-arounds for Falafel. They are very much like English muffins in texture. The Mexican tortilla, made of cornmeal and baked while you wait, is perhaps the nearest familiar equivalent.

1 teaspoon granular yeast	2 cups all-purpose flour
¼ cup warm water	⅛ teaspoon salt
1 teaspoon sugar	3 tablespoons cooking oil
1 egg, beaten	⅓ cup lukewarm water

Dissolve the yeast in lukewarm water and add sugar to stimulate yeast action. Add egg. Sift together flour and salt and stir in yeast mixture, adding oil and lukewarm water gradually while stirring to form a soft dough. Cover and let rise at room temperature till double in bulk. Form into 12 flat cakes and place on a lightly greased and floured shallow baking pan. Let rise till light, about double in bulk. Flatten lightly with the fingers or prick with a fork. Brush with water or oil. Bake 20 minutes at 375° or till lightly browned. These soft flat rolls should be about 3 or 4 inches in diameter and puffed so that there is a hollow in the center. The dough requires no kneading.

Serve hot from the oven with freshly made Falafel or main dishes.

Yields 12.

NAHIT SAUCE

1 cup cooked *nahit* (chick peas)	⅛ teaspoon powdered garlic
½ cup liquid	4 tablespoons peanut oil or sesame seed oil (Tahini)

Drain the cooked *nahit* which should be tender enough to mash with a fork. Mash well and add the liquid in which the peas were cooked. Season with garlic and add a pinch of salt if necessary. Work in the peanut oil or Tahini (can be purchased at Greek food shops or Jewish food stores which import cans of shortening from Israel) and serve with salads, as a sauce for broiled meats or poultry or with vegetable dishes, especially eggplant.

Four tablespoons peanut butter may be used if Tahini is not available. Work in till smooth.

Yields 1 pint sauce.

ISRAEL EGGPLANT DISHES

The eggplant was at one time called the Dead Sea Apple. It is used for a large variety of dishes and no meal in Israel is considered complete without some form of eggplant on the menu. Below are a few of the favorite ways of preparing this versatile vegetable so popular with both the native-born Israelis and immigrants from the Near Eastern countries and the west as well as Europe.

CHEESE AND EGGPLANT

(Egyptian Jews call this dish Patlijan Boereg.)

1 large ripe eggplant	3 eggs
1 teaspoon salt	½ pound dry pot cheese
¼ cup sifted flour	1 teaspoon minced parsley
¾ cup cooking oil	1 tablespoon lemon juice

Wash and slice unpared eggplant into ¼-inch rounds. Sprinkle lightly with salt and let stand approximately half an hour. Pat each slice dry, dust lightly with flour and fry in hot oil (or melted vegetable shortening) till nicely browned on both sides. Pour off excess oil or shortening, leaving the fried eggplant in the frying pan. Beat 2 eggs, add dry pot cheese and minced parsley, mixing well. Spread over the fried eggplant in the pan, lifting some of the slices over the eggs and cheese mixture. Cover and cook over low heat for 3 to 5 minutes. Beat remaining egg till frothy. Lift cover and pour the beaten egg over all. Cook uncovered only till set. Serve hot garnished with minced parsley and a sprinkling of lemon juice.

Serves 4 to 6.

EGGPLANT WITH EGGS AND ONIONS (Basic Recipe)

1 large eggplant, pared and diced	¼ teaspoon salt
2 medium-size onions, sliced thin	2 tablespoons grated Cheddar-type
3 tablespoons cooking oil	cheese
4 to 6 eggs	parsley or fresh dill

Sprinkle the cubed eggplant with salt and let stand while frying the sliced onion in hot oil till light yellow or a golden brown. Rinse and pat dry the eggplant and add to the fried onion in the pan. Cover and cook over low heat until eggplant is tender but not cooked apart and mushy, approximately 10 minutes. Remove cover and shake frying pan to prevent sticking. Beat eggs—allowing one egg per serving, season with a little salt and turn over the contents of pan. Cook only till the eggs are set but not dry. Turn out on a heated serving plate or platter and sprinkle grated cheese and minced greens on top for garnish.

Serves 4 to 6.

MARINATED EGGPLANT, for Meat or Fish Dishes

4 small eggplants per serving	1 onion, sliced thin, per serving
cold water as directed	bay leaves, peppercorns or mixed
salt to taste	whole spice
cider or wine vinegar, diluted to	1 tablespoon dark brown sugar
taste	(optional)

Small eggplants are best for this purpose but large ones may be used. Cut into 2-inch lengths, not more than an inch thick. Do not pare. Add enough cold water to prevent scorching and bring to a boil. Add salt to taste and cook 5 to 10 minutes or till tender but not cooked apart. Drain well. Dilute vinegar with the liquid and add sliced onion, bay leaves, peppercorns or whole mixed spices. Add sugar if desired, and bring to a boil. Place the drained eggplant in an earthenware container and pour the hot mixture over to cover. Cover and store about 2 weeks before serving with meat or fish dishes.

SAVORY EGGPLANT

2 pounds eggplant	1 cup strained tomato sauce
¼ cup sifted flour or dry crumbs	(fresh or canned)
6 tablespoons cooking oil	6 tablespoons dry crumbs
2 onions, chopped fine	a dash of salt
	a pinch of ground ginger
	(optional)

Slice unpared eggplant into ½-inch-thick slices. Dip each slice in flour and fry in hot cooking oil till browned on both sides. Chop or mash the fried egg plant, add chopped onions, tomato sauce, and sprinkle with crumbs to cover. Sprinkle with salt and ginger, if used, and turn into a greased baking dish or casserole. The fat in frying pan will be sufficient on top of the mixture. May be sprinkled with additional dry crumbs if desired. Bake 20 to 30 minutes at 350°, depending on depth of contents in baking dish. The onions should be well cooked and the top nicely browned.

Serves 6.

ISRAEL FRUIT SOUP (Basic Recipe)

2 cups fresh or frozen berries of
  any kind
1 quart cold water, skimmed
  milk or sour milk

sugar or honey to sweeten to taste
lemon or orange juice to taste
  (optional)
1 tablespoon sour cream per
  serving

Put the berries through a strainer, leaving a few for floating on top of each serving of the chilled soup. Stir in all ingredients except sour cream and serve cold, chilled in the refrigerator for at least 1 hour before serving. Stir in sour cream or float on top of each serving and decorate with a few whole berries.

Serves 6 to 8.

POTATO DOUGH FRUIT DUMPLINGS (Basic Recipe)

1 cup warm mashed potatoes
1 egg

flour to make a firm dough
1/8 teaspoon grated lemon or orange
  rind

Work the ingredients together in a mixing bowl to form a dough firm enough to mold or pat out to 1/2-inch thickness. Use a small cookie cutter for the patted-out dough, if desired. A thimble can be used to cut out tiny rounds. Drop these in deep melted vegetable shortening or cooking oil and fry till lightly browned. Or arrange on a greased cookie sheet and bake 8 minutes at 350° or till lightly browned.

Serves 2 to 4.

UNCOOKED FRUIT PUDDING (Israel Specialty)

For Sabbath or holidays, when cooking is forbidden, an easy-to-prepare and serve pudding is served as directed below. It is then stored in the refrigerator until serving time and spooned out with a large serving spoon into sauce dishes. It is further garnished with fresh berries, chopped nuts or sprinkled with shredded coconut. It serves as a dessert dish with either *fleishig* or *milchig* meals.

Spread a layer of fresh berries or stewed dried fruit in the bottom of a pudding dish or bowl. Sprinkle generously with sugar and chopped nuts, a little grated lemon or orange rind or a dash of cinnamon. Arrange toasted bread sliced or diced over this and cover with the same combination of fresh berries (or frozen kind) and sprinkle with chopped nuts, raisins and flavorings. Cover with more toasted bread and repeat till the bowl is filled to within an inch of the top. Pour in enough fresh or frozen (diluted or full strength) orange juice and let stand overnight in the refrigerator.

INDEX